Meet Jakob Lorber

fragments from a Christian teaching

taken from the book "The Great Gospel of John", written by Jakob Lorber between 1851 and 1864.

Author: Marius Petre
Editor: Agela Mayer

This synthesis was done based on the original German book *"Das grosse Evangelium Johannes"*, written by Jakob Lorber between 1851 and 1864.

© Marius Petre.
For contact use mpetre70@gmail.com

TABLE OF CONTENTS

1	**GOD AND THE CREATION**	**19**
1.1	THE PRIMORDIAL SOURCE	19
1.2	ABOUT THE TRINITY	22
1.3	THE TWO POLES	29
1.4	ABOUT JESUS CHRIST	32
1.5	THE CREATION	39
1.6	SPACE AND TIME	50
1.7	HEAVEN AND EARTH	54
1.8	THE KINGDOM OF HEAVEN	59
1.9	SEVEN DIVINE ATTRIBUTES	65
1.10	THE WAR BETWEEN HEAVEN AND EARTH	68
1.11	ANGELS, MEN AND DEVILS	72
2	**ABOUT MEN**	**75**
2.2	BODY, SOUL AND SPIRIT	78
2.3	ABOUT SPIRITUAL DEVELOPMENT	85
2.4	THE PERFECT HUMAN BEING	93
2.5	TWO CATEGORIES OF HUMAN SOULS	95
2.6	THE RIGHT SPIRITUAL GUIDANCE	99
3	**ABOUT ANGELS**	**104**
3.1	THE GUARDIAN ANGELS	106
3.2	ABOUT LIFE AND SEXUALITY OF ANGELS	108
3.3	ANGELS AND HUMANS	110
4	**ABOUT DEVILS**	**115**
4.1	ABOUT LUCIFER	119

4.2	ABOUT SATAN	129
4.3	ABOUT DIFFERENT KIND OF HELLS	132
4.4	JUDAS ISCARIOT	136

5	**LIFE AND DEATH**	**141**
5.1	IN THE BEGINNING…	141
5.2	LIFE AS IT IS!	143
5.3	ABOUT NUTRITION	148
5.4	CLEANSING THE TEMPLE	153
5.5	ABOUT SEXUALITY	157
5.6	ABOUT DEATH AND THE LIFE IN THE BEYOND	162
5.7	ABOUT RE-INCARNATION	174

6	**THE METHOD**	**179**
6.1	THE TEACHING	179
6.2	LOVE GOD ABOVE ALL!	189
6.3	ABOUT FREEDOM	191
6.4	ABOUT FREEWILL	196
6.5	ABOUT DISCIPLES	204
6.6	THE GORDIAN KNOT	206
6.7	SCIENCE AND FAITH	207
6.8	ABOUT THE WILL POWER	210
6.9	TO BE BORN AGAIN	212
6.10	THE MISSING LINK	215

7	**THE PRACTICE**	**221**
7.1	ABOUT VIRTUE AND VICE	221
7.2	ABOUT BEING ACTIVE	224
7.3	NOTHING BUT THE TRUTH	229
7.4	ABOUT SERVICE	230
7.5	ABOUT HUMILITY	232
7.6	ABOUT MERCY	239

7.7	About repent and confession	240
7.8	About real strength	242
7.9	About faith	246
7.10	About revelation and the true prophet	247
7.11	Why to return good for evil?	250
7.12	About clairvoyance through introspection	252
7.13	About praying	255
7.14	About fasting	260
7.15	The hearers and the doers	262

INTRODUCTION

What would you say, if I told you that Einstein was not the first one in the West who wrote about the unity of space and time? What would you think, if I told you that, in respect with the nature of the Universe and man, the most complex and profound metaphysical system[1] was created in the 19th century by Jakob Lorber, and since then almost completely disregarded by all mainstream Western thinkers?

Jakob Lorber declared he wrote his books through divine dictation, meaning he heard a voice in his heart, which told him what to write in his books. In their effort to convince us it must have been a divine dictation, his admirers described him as a simple but educated man without too many books in his home, nor any other easy access to information.

My decision to write the book you are now holding in your hands - based entirely on the book "The Great Gospel of John" written by Jakob Lorber - wasn't taken having in mind the divine dictation. From my point of view, the source of Lorber's inspiration is not important, because that was a fundamentally subjective experience. In Lorber's terms, the subjective religious experience should be balanced by a scientific approach towards the outside world, because in this way we could better understand the miracle of life. This life includes the inner life, as well! Science is meant to free man from heathenism, which is just a primitive and (or) a fanatic religious thinking. Therefore, I think Lorber's book speaks for itself, and the discussion around

---

[1] Metaphysics is a branch of philosophy concerned with explaining the fundamental nature of being and the world.

the source of Lorber's inspiration makes no difference: his ideas are more important then everything else!

Plus, the ones who are arguing that Lorber was an "uncomplicated man", as his biographer and friend Karl Gottfried Ritter von Leitner described him, aren't making much sense, because anyone who has a little bit of spirit could read between the lines of his "official" biography. Lorber was an educated man, he studied in Gratz and he became a musician, who learnt his art from Paganini and played on the most famous and prestigious stage of his time, Scala di Milano. Now, we all know that musicians are generally complicated people, usually having a lot of friends and enemies, and Lorber should have been the same.

Anyhow, if you take the time to read "The Great Gospel of John", which is a torrent book (the original German book has ten volumes, each having around 240 chapters!), and you have some background readings of the works of his predecessors, like the Christian writer Jakob Böhme, or the mystic Emanuel Swedenborg (Lorber himself made a reference to Swedenborg, in his book *From Hell to Heaven* – second volume, chapter 104, verse 4) it will become obvious for you that he is using the same terminology as them, in respect with what is called the metaphysical realm.

Those who do not believe the divine dictation story are using these facts to say that God is not speaking in mystical concepts nor Lorber was in contact with a deity, but with the work of his predecessors, and therefore his books cannot be considered as gospel.

In my opinion, both these groups are basically wrong, because instead of talking about the book and its ideas, they are arguing about its source of inspiration. They don't see the forest for the trees! When one is focusing too much on a single issue, one has a good chance to miss the big picture.

Which in my opinion reads as following: "The Great Gospel of John" is arguably the most unlikely book ever written!

Let me explain why I believe that!

The most unlikely book ever!

If you want to learn about the humanity's efforts in building explanatory systems, meant to offer an understanding of the world and our part in it, then you will have to look at the thinkers living in the Indian continent, the ones living around Himalayan Mountains, the Chinese, the Japanese, the European thinkers, the ancient Egyptians, the Jews, the Arabs, etc.

Now, if we will try to look at these efforts taking into account the scope of their theories and the depth of their arguments, we could see that almost all these systems appear as more or less underdeveloped, when they are compared with Kashmiri Shaivism (Pratyabijna School)[2]. This system is the work of a series of highly educated spiritual masters, during hundreds of years. It was, for me, the most complex and the most profound metaphysical system I ever encountered. Until I met Lorber!

---

[2] Kashmiri Shaivism arose during the eighth or ninth century CE. in Kashmiri and made significant strides, both philosophical and theological, until the end of the twelfth century. Kashmiri Shaivism is based on a strong monistic interpretation of the *Bhairava Tantras* (and its subcategory the *Kaula Tantras*). The forefathers of the Kashmiri Shaivism are the following: Somananda, the first theologian of monistic Shaivism, who was the teacher of Utpaladeva, who was the grand-teacher of Abhinava Gupta, who in turn was the teacher of Ksemaraja.

When I am referring to the complexity of a metaphysical system, I think about covering almost all the basic questions about the Universe and about us. Namely: Is there anybody responsible for the creation of the Universe? What is the fabric of the Universe and its building blocks? What is its purpose, if there is any? What are its laws and how does it function? What is space and what is time? From where are we coming and where are we going? Is there anybody responsible for our creation? What is the structure a human being and which are our building blocks? What is the relation between us and the Universe?

It is important to highlight that I am not looking at these systems in search for the Truth; I am just trying to see if there is any wisdom in them! Namely, I am interested to see if these systems are coming with intelligent answers to all these important questions, and their answers are sound and useful, and in line with the scientific data at hand.

Every system I looked into (and I studied both the well known Western systems as well as the Eastern systems) was either partial, or with a more-or-less fable argumentation. With one notable exception: the Kashmiri Shaivism (which became known to the West long after Lorber death!). After I read "The Great Gospel of John" I realized I've found a similarly complex and sound explanatory system. Which, in its main points (God, Creation, the human being) is even more interesting then Kashmiri Shaivism!

So, what several spiritual masters created in hundreds of years having Hindu philosophy as foundation, Lorber accomplished on its own, in only 13 years, having Christian theology as foundation! And that is exactly why I earlier labeled this as "the most unlikely book ever!"

Let me repeat myself: I don't think the source of his inspiration is what matters (being divine or from human mind), only the result: a sound explanatory system, more complex and more interesting than everything the brightest of the human thinkers have ever produced!

What you will find in this book?

Lorber's book is written by a Christian, and therefore it is a Christian religious book. For a reader who is not Christian, and/or who does not believe in this so-called divine dictation, it is quite difficult to digest thousands of pages that read like a fantasy saga.

This book is difficult to be accepted even for a Christian who believes in the divine dictation, because it brings ideas which are very far from the accepted Christian doctrine. Surely, these could be couple of reasons why the book is so overlooked by mainstream Western thinkers!

Another reason why this book is so underrated could stem from the fact that the narrative contains three different threads, which are constantly overlapping.

One is describing what supposedly the daily life of Jesus was, the second one portraits Jesus effort to convince his followers, consequently the readers, that he is Christ, while the third is describing an explanatory system for the Universe, the man and their interconnections.

These overlapping subjects are making the reader's task very difficult and the brilliant metaphysical system developed by Lorber ended hidden by religious quotations and the storyline of Jesus" life.

The metaphysical system is the one that deeply impressed me, and this is the main reason I wrote this book: it was done in an effort to share with my friends some of the most interesting parts of the amazing metaphysical system developed by Lorber.

When I first decided to write this book, I wanted to synthesize the whole system in one book. After a while, I realized I would have needed volumes, which wasn't in my plan at all!

Therefore, I wrote this as a trailer, to awaken your curiosity about Jakob Lorber amazing achievement, and to entice you with some his wonderful ideas that are the essence of his wonderful system. That's why I kept the format of the text as in his books and translated it as accurately as possible. Since my book is nevertheless a synthesis, I grouped the ideas by subject and cleaned the text of any collateral information.

The ones, who are interested to understand all the subtleties of Lorber's thinking, would have to read his book, "The Great Gospel of John". My book is a presentation of the main aspects of this system and by reading it I hope you will find the necessary motivation to approach Lorber's work. As in incentive, let me give you some interesting examples from his metaphysical system.

For Lorber, Jesus was a milestone in the worldwide development of religions. He said that before Jesus, the most profound religious movements, like Buddhism, Hinduism and Taoism, were referring to an impersonal God, who exists beyond space and eternity. In true, for Hinduism there is Brahman, the Absolute, the one from whom everything is coming and where everything will end up going, including Brahma, the Creator. For Buddhism everything is in its essence impersonal, non-self. For Taoism there is Tao, the one without a form, without a name, the first cause and the last home for everything and everyone.

In Lorber's opinion, all of the above are profound but limited perspectives on God and the Universe. He said that Jesus came to teach us how to fully develop our spirit (the re-birth of our spirit), while the previous religions were helping us fully develop our soul (the re-birth of the soul). In his opinion, after you discover the limitless and impersonal aspect of God, which represents the birth of your spirit, you have to move further to develop this spirit by interacting with the personal aspect of God, which he called Light, the Primordial Cause.

For old religions, God is the One, prior to all existence, immovable, abiding in the solitude of His own unity. From that Absolute existence, at a certain point, the Supreme God arises, the Source of all things, the First Cause, unfolding Himself into all existences. For Lorber, Jesus came to teach us that there is no instance when the One, called the Absolute, was alone, without its Light, called the Supreme Creator. He says that the One and its Light exist altogether, therefore the Light is not created at a certain point, but it is the continuous and personal manifestation of the One, the Absolute.

Interestingly enough, the old religions never found a solution to the problem of the identity of the spirit, which it is said that lays in every human being. If the One is alone, at the beginning and at the end, then my own spirit has only an ephemeral individuality. If at the end my free enlightened spirit will have the slightest individual trait, then the One is not the One anymore, but a collection of multiple spirits. This dilemma gave headaches to all the old wise men. They tried and failed to solve it, and Bhagavad Gita is just one of such failed attempts. Therefore, even today, two groups exist in respect with this matter: one, which is arguing there is just One Spirit, which lays in every one of us, but they failed to explain how come this spirit is still chained in me, and freed in Krishna, or Buddha.

The other is saying there is an individual spirit in every one of us, but they failed to explain how, in the end, the One and the Different will exist together, beyond space and time.

Lorber's answer to this dilemma is simple: the One and its Light existed together from always, and in this and from this Light we all took our individual spirit, which will remain individual in this Light, for eternity and beyond.

As I said, Lorber argued that Jesus was a milestone in the development of religions, and he said that after Jesus, all the religions have taken a step further in their understanding of God, the Universe and man. Since that actually happened, it looks like Lorber was just examining the facts, but in reality he had no access to these facts.

Two examples: Around 11th century AD, the Kashmiri Shaivism, which represents the development of the old Hindu tradition, talks about Bhairava Shiva (God) as Prakasha-Vimarsha (Consciousness and its Light). The Tibetan Buddhism, in its Vajrayana branch, which probably came into existence in the 6th or 7th century AD[3] and represents the development of the Buddhist tradition, moved forward from the pure non-self, impersonal existence and it talked about the Clear Light, which is achieved by practicing different meditation techniques.

In conclusion I think it is quite impressive that a German writer, in the 19th century, without access to either Kashmiri Shaivism, or Vajrayana (both become popular in the West starting with the end of the 19th century and beginning of the 20th century!), was able to see and write about this trend in the development of religions.

---

[3] Akira, Hirakawa (1993), Paul Groner, ed., *History of Indian Buddhism*, Delhi: Motilal Banarsidass Publishers

About Jakob Lorber[4]

Jakob Lorber was born on July 22, 1800, in Kanischa, parish of Jahring, in the Austrian province of lower Styria, which today is part of the Republic of Slovenia. His peasant family was not very rich, and open to art and religion.

Jakob inherited his father's musical talent and learned to play violin, piano and organ. This helped him later to pay for his education, first in Marburg and then in Graz, the Styrian capital, where in 1829 he obtained his diploma as a teacher for intermediate schools.

When he could not find a suitable position, he reverted to his particular love, music. He gave lessons in singing and the violin, he take lessons from the virtuoso violinist Paganini, practiced for hours every day, composed and sometimes gave concerts, alone or together with others, and once he played a violin concert at the La Scala Opera House, in Milan. He was successful, but never to the extent he hoped for.

During all these years he followed his penchant towards spirituality, coming into contact with the works of Justinus Kerner, Jung-Stilling, Emmanuel Swedenborg, Jakob Böhme and Johann Tennhardt.

Finally, when he was offered the post as conductor at the opera, in Trieste, promising to greatly improve his financial situation, he received his life call, which he labeled: "scribe of the Lord". Early that morning of March 15, 1840 he heard an

---

[4] This part was taken from different internet sources which are dedicated to Jakob Lorber.

inner voice in his heart, commanding: "Get up, take your pen and write!"

Putting his newly found job aside, he sat down and dutifully wrote what the mysterious voice dictated. It was the introduction to his first work, "The Household of God". This first hour changed Lorber's life entirely. For the following 24 years, his remaining lifetime, he rarely interrupted his activity. He sat for hours, almost daily, without consulting books or libraries during his work. Obeying his inner voice became the sense of his life.

It is important for the reader to understand how this so-called inspiration through the inner word it is said that works. Lorber wasn't a medium of automatic writing, whose hand is guided by some sort of spirit-entity, or however it is called. Fully awake, he said he was hearing a voice in his heart and promptly wrote down what he heard. That means his inspiration was filtered through his mind, and then recorded in words of human language. In his case, as in any other cases, his book expresses always his particular manner of thinking and speaking.

From a religious perspective, Lorber explained the divine dictation as following : "The Lord (Jesus) said: Whoever wants to talk with me, should come to me and I will put the answer into his heart, but only the pure whose heart is humble shall hear the sound of my voice. And who prefers me before the entire world, loves me like the bride her groom, with him I shall walk arm in arm. He will always perceive me like one brother the other and like I perceived him since eternity, even before he came into being."

At the time of his calling, this simple man probably didn't suspect that writing would keep him busy for 24 years. This work, contained in 24 books of almost 500 pages each, not to mention a number of shorter writings, presents an amazing phenomenon with the comprehensive ideas they contain, the deep interpretations and amazing paradigm on the subject of cosmology, astronomy, biology, natural science, psychology and Christianity.

Lorber was open and friendly in respect with his transcriptions and he was observed while writing by well-educated men, such as Dr. Carl-Friedrich Zimpel, the mayor of Graz, Anton Hüttenbrenner, his brother the composer Anselm Hüttenbrenner, the poet and Secretary of State Karl Gottfried von Leitner, Leopold Cantily, a pharmacist of Graz, and others. [5]

Lorber's greatest and best known work, written during the years 1851 to 1864, is "The Great Gospel of John", in 10 volumes. It begins with an explanation of the Biblical gospel according to St. John and then gives a detailed account of the three teaching years of Jesus, revealing what could be called a full Christian teaching. This teaching looks so complete and comprehensive, that if one consider it the real teaching which was taught by Jesus two thousand years ago, then one could easily understand the immense impact it had during the life of Jesus and afterwards.

This literature will speak for itself for the reader with an open and incisive mind, who has the honest desire to study the explanatory system conceptualized by Lorber, which tries to offer some answers to almost all the questions that forever puzzled mankind.

From a traditional point of view, Lorber would have to be characterized in superlatives. As a man of letters he surpasses all authors, poets and thinkers of all time. In my opinion, there is no

---

[5] In „The Prophet J. Lorber Predicts Coming Catastrophies and the True Christianity" by Kurt Eggenstein

word to correctly characterize him. He described himself, humbly, just as: "scribe servant of God".

Lorber died on August 24, 1864. His tombstone reads the words of St. Paul: "In life or in death, we all belong to the Lord!"

Nota bene

Even though appears as such, the scope of this work is not the propagation of religious believes. Nowadays, more and more people are trying to find something or someone who could give them the key, or show them the path to a fulfilled life. Of course, there are numerous perspectives on what a fulfilled life should be, and therefore the world is now full of enterprises trying to respond to such a demand.

In my opinion, a very interesting part of life is to find useful answers to your fundamental questions, which basically implies only three things: firstly, these questions should really belong to you; secondly, you should continuously apply yourself to finding these answers; ultimately, to get results, you have to keep an open mind and an intuitive heart.

Lorber's book helped me find some of my answers.

I hope it will offer you the same opportunity!

1 GOD AND THE CREATION

1.1 The Primordial Source

The primordial essence, the primal cause (of all life), is Light (the great holy creative will, the primal existential idea). The light is the substantially visible God and is thus not only in, but also with God and, as it is, flow around the Divine Being.

Who or what actually is this Light, this great will, this most holly fundamental idea of all future substantial, utterly free existence? It could not possibly be anything else but God Himself, since God, through God, and nothing but God Himself could manifest it in His eternally, most perfect being. That means the Light doesn't come to an existence, and therefore it will not vanish in eternity, but it is beyond time and existence, and the highest form of God.

The Light sets its eternal idea of creation, out of itself into a tangible, visible existence, and there is nothing in the entire eternal infinity that did not go forth from the Light, the First Cause, in the same way assuming a manifest and visible existence.

It is obvious that the First Cause of all existence, the light of lights, the original thought of all thoughts and ideas, the archetype as the eternal original form of all forms, firstly, could not be formless and, secondly, could not be dead, since death signifies the very opposite to all existence in whatever form. Thus there was a most perfect life in this Light, or in this great thought within fundamentally God Himself. So God was from eternity the most perfect fundamental life in and out of Himself, through and through, and this Light or life called forth out of itself all created beings, and this light or life was the light and also the life within all the creatures, within the human beings as well. Thus, these creatures and human beings are a complete part of the Primordial Light, which gave them their existence, light, and a life very similar to the eternal primordial existence.

The primordial life in God is and must be a perfectly free life; otherwise, it would be as good as no life at all. This same life must be one and the same life in the created beings; otherwise, it would not be life and, thus, without life also would be without existence. It is obvious that the created beings – men – could only be given a completely free life, which has to be aware of itself as a complete life, but also have to realize that it is not a life that had come forth from itself, but had come forth as fully equal out of God, in accordance with His eternally almighty will.

At the beginning, this perception had to be present in all created beings, just as the one that their life and existence must be completely equal to the Life of God, as otherwise they would not have any life or existence.

When we consider this circumstance more closely, it becomes evident that these two feelings meet in the created beings. Namely, in the first place, the feeling of equality with God, or the presence of God's primordial light within them, and then, as resulting from this light, also the feeling of having been created at some time through the primordial will of the Creator.

The first feeling makes the created being equal to the Creator and, therefore, completely independent of the eternal First Cause. The second vital feeling, necessarily arising from the first, must still consider and regard itself as having been called forth from the actual First Cause, an only in the course of time freely manifested being, and thus most dependent on the First Cause.

Now, this humbling realization turns the initial feeling of exaltation also into a feeling of humility, which for the exaltation is a most necessary and desirable matter, as will be plainly shown hereinafter.

The feeling of exaltation puts up a mighty resistance to such humiliation and wants to avoid it completely. Such a conflict then causes anger and finally hate against the First Cause of all that exists and resulting from that against the lowly feeling of humility and dependence, whereupon the feeling of exaltation becomes weak and benighted and the primal light within the created being gives way to night and darkness. With this night and this darkness inside, the created being become then almost unable to recognize the primal light within itself and, as almost blind, but still independent, distances itself from the First Cause of its existence and creation, unable to recognize the same in its delusion.

Therefore, the primordial light may shine in such night as brightly as it may, but since the night is no longer able to see properly, it does not recognize the light, which is coming into such night in order to transform it, once more, into the true original and aware light.

Also, this primordial light is the eternally great glory in God, and God Himself is this glory. This glory was from eternity God Himself within God, and all being have received their existence and their light and independent life from the fullness of this glory. Thus all life is a grace of God filling the life-bearing form through and through.

Since this first grace within the created being was in danger of being completely lost, the primordial light itself came into the world and taught people to completely return into this primal existence, to receive a new life for the old light. And this exchange is the receiving of grace upon grace or the giving away of the old, weakened, quite useless life for anew, imperishable life in and from god in all fullness.

The first grace was a necessity in which there is neither freedom nor permanence. But the second grace is complete freedom without any compulsion and, therefore, since not urged or coerced by anything, also forever indestructible. For where there is no enemy, there is also no destruction. (By enemy is to be understood all that in any way impedes a free existence.)

1.2 *About the Trinity*

God is in Spirit always the same, thus forever and in Himself unchangeable, for in Him, as the most endless perfection, no further change is conceivable. God is the only and everlasting primordial source of all being. Everything which exists is nothing else than His deeds; therefore, their being is also a God-being, and their life is God-life.

In God everything is the fullest, everlasting truth, because nothing can be anywhere outside God. Therefore, we are also in God, but we are aware about this only as far as we are one with His holiest Spirit, through our love for Him. The pure love for God connects us with Him and makes us one with Him; and because of that, everything become purest light, wherever we might turn to. This primordial light in its highest purity of the spirit is then the very everlasting, unchangeable truth.

But the endless glory of God does not have the power – and it is impossible to have it! – to create Gods outside of Himself, who are completely equal to Him. For if He would be able to do that, He would be able to create one endless universe beside other equally endless universe, which any clearly thinking person can already see it from a distance that this is the purest nonsense. For if the first universe is endless in all imaginable directions, then where must the second equally endless universe begin?

A second perfect God with the fullest endless glory is therefore quite as unimaginable as a second endless universe.

If God could creates more Gods, like for instance the Son and the Holy Spirit, so that the two would be individually different from Him, then they inevitably could claim all His unlimited power, without which no God could be imagined, no more than one can imagine a second or even third endless universe that would be divided in a certain way, limiting each other. However, if this would be thinkable, then what about God's sovereignty of which there can only be one?

The one Kingdom of the one God can exist eternally because only He is the only King and Lord of it, as it is written in the books of the prophets, who have prophesized out of the mouth of God: "God will give His glory to no one else" (Isaiah 42:8).

Human beings, Angels, Dominions and Powers, all things in Heaven and on all globes have always bowed before God and will throughout eternity only bow before Him and never for anybody else.

If by the names Father, Son and Holy Spirit, not one self-existing God – the one Primordial Being – has to be understood, and instead of that a Son that is separated from the Father, and likewise a different Holy Spirit would be accepted, then what kind of God would the Father be?

If there exist a Son and a Holy Spirit, who are different from the Father and would exist besides Himself, as it is the case with angels and human beings, then they can be nothing else but His created beings, because they did not receive their being – no matter how perfect it may be – of themselves, as a result of their very own and eternal perfect power, but only from the one Creator.

However, how can there be a complete, divine relationship or a real unity between a spirit without body and form and a spirit with body and form? Can it be said that the Son – who is a bodily Person – is in the Father if the Father has no body, no shape and no form? Or can the infinite Father, without having a body, shape and form, be in the Son?

Moreover: if the Holy Spirit is a third person as such, coming from the Father and the Son, then how can that person have the same qualities as those two are having and who are equally eternal? Can eternity ever be equal to the all-fleeing time, or the limited area to infinity?

Even if one can accept that all the times of times are contained in eternity and are moving and changing, then it is however impossible to think and assert that time, no matter how long it lasts, can comprise eternity. Just like one can also think and assert that the endless primordial space surely can contain all spaces – which, no matter how big they may be, are finally still limited – but these last ones can impossible contain the primordial space.

Now, if you understand the idea of not accepting three gods as such, then you learn that these "3 persons" are in fact three attributes of God. The Father, the Son and the Holy Spirit are distinguishable one and the same from eternity. The Father is the everlasting love and as such the primordial reason and the actual primordial substance of all things, which fills the whole of eternity.

The Son is the light and wisdom, which goes forth from the fire of everlasting love. This mighty light is the everlasting most perfect self-consciousness and the brightest self-recognition of God and is the everlasting Word in God, through which everything there is has been created.

The mightiest will of God is the very Holy Spirit, through which the works and beings obtain their fullest existence. The Holy Spirit is the great pronounced word: "It shall be!" And it is what the love and wisdom in God have decided.

One could find the same trilogy in itself. Every person has love in him and according to such love also a will; since love in itself is a desire and longing, and in this desire and longing lays the actual will.

Even the most uneducated and coarsest person possesses love and will. But what does he do with it? He satisfies only the lowest and most physical needs, which instinctively translates from his raw love to his will, from which his mind obtains nothing else than a dark haze. Look at the works of such people, if they are not many times worse than those produced by animals, whose love and desire is guided by a higher influence!

However, it is completely different with the love and its will of those people, whose mind has become a bright light; it penetrates the love, its wisdom and thereby the whole person. Only now does love provides the pure means, the light or wisdom orders it, and the will turns it into action.

The human has been created totally in God's image, and whoever wants to know himself completely must realize that as one and the same human being he actually also consists of three aspects. We firstly have a form, provided of all the necessary senses and other parts from very big to hardly unimaginably small, which are necessary for a free and independent life. This form has, for the benefit of the development of the soul, its own very natural life within that is different in every respect from the spiritual life of the soul.

For example, the physical body lives on material food of which the blood and the other nutritious juices are formed for the different parts of the body. With these activities of life, the soul has nothing to do with it, because this activity has no connection with the free will of the soul, no more than a person has something to do with the very activity of their lungs, the liver, the spleen, the stomach, the intestines, the kidneys, and so much more countless parts of his body.

The soul must have an outer form, because of a certain existence, namely that of a human being. Consequently, the outer form is that which we call the body or also the flesh, be it still material or spiritualized substantial, no matter how.

If we consider now only the soul, then we will see that also he is in himself entirely a complete human being, who has a spiritual substance also in himself and for the benefit of himself precisely the same parts as the body, and in a higher, spiritual respect he is using them just like the body is using his material parts.

Now, although the body on the one hand and the soul on the other hand represent two totally different human beings or persons, of who each has his own individual activity, they finally cannot even understand the how and why of those activities, and they are in the light of the actual purpose of life nevertheless only one human being.

Consequently, nobody can claim that he is not an individual but a twofold human being, because the body must serve the soul, and this one, with his reason and will, must serve the body. And consequently, the soul is equally responsible for the acts for which he has made use of the body, as well as for his very own acts that exist of all kinds of thoughts, wishes, desires and lusts.

When we however consider more in detail the life of the soul as such, we soon will discover that also he is a substantial bodily being, who in himself stands not much higher than at best for instance the soul of an ape. Although he possesses an instinctive thinking-faculty of a somewhat higher level than a simple animal, an intellect and a higher free opinion about certain things and their interrelation would be out of the question.

This higher potential in the soul that is in fact the highest and equal to God comes from a pure essential, spiritual, third human being, who lives in the soul, the Spirit. Through him, he can distinguish that which is true from the false and that which is good from the evil, and is able to think freely in all imaginable directions and is able to will in complete freedom. As he –the Spirit – will direct himself with his free will towards that which is purely true and good, he slowly, in the same proportion, will make himself completely equal with the Divine Spirit of God.

When this is the case, the soul is becoming one with his Spirit and will be completely changed into the spiritual substantial body, which you can call the reborn in the soul. Finally, the soul will also be changed into the essential body of the Spirit, under which the true resurrection of the flesh has to be understood as the true day of the life of the soul, which begins when a man is completely reborn in the spirit, be it already here in this life or – what will cost some more trouble and time – in the beyond.

In the spirit, or the eternal essence, lives love, as the all-accomplishing power, the highest wisdom and the living firm will. All this together brings about the substance of the soul and gives him his form or being of the body.

Even though a completely reborn man in the spirit is only one perfect human being, his being exists nevertheless in himself eternally out of a well distinguishable trinity.

With every thing and every object there is a distinguishable trinity. What will strike the eye first is of course the outer form, for without this nothing and no object or being could have any existence. And when the first exists, the second one is of course the content of the existent things and objects, for without this, they also could not exist and they also could not have any form or outer shape. Now what is the third, which is as necessary for the existence of a being or object as the first and the second one? That is an inner power that keeps the content of the being or objects thoroughly together and which forms their actual existence. And since this power consists of the content and consequently also of the outer form, it is also the original life of all that exists, no matter of what kind its nature may be. And without this power, the existence of a being or thing or object would be quite as unimaginable as without content and without an outer form.

We can see now that the three mentioned parts are as such easy to be distinguished, since the outer form is not its content and the content is not its inherent power. And still, these parts are completely one, because if there would be no power, there would be no content and certainly also no form.

Thus, once the soul of the human being is present – according to the will and the intelligence of the spirit – the spirit withdraws itself deep into the center and gives the now existing soul according to its deepest inner will and intelligence a free will that is as it were separated from it, and a free, as it were independent intelligence that the soul can, partly by his outer sense-organs and partly by an inner capability of perception acquire to himself and perfect it as if it would be completely the very own work of this completely free intelligence.

As a result of this condition that is formed by necessity in which he feels as it were separated from his spirit, the soul is capable to receive an outer as well as an inner revelation. If he receives it, accepts and acts according to it, he will also by that become one with his spirit and therefore will more and more come to the unlimited freedom of the spirit, not only with regard to the intelligence and the freedom of will according to this enlightened intelligence, but also in the power and the might to accomplish everything whatever he recognizes and wills.

Again, from this you can see that the soul – as the thought of the spirit that has changed into living substance, which is actually the spirit itself – can still in a certain way be considered as something that came forth as second from the spirit, without being something else, except the spirit itself.

The fact that finally the soul becomes visible as an individual, clothed with an outer body that in a certain way appears as a third personality, is shown to you by daily experience. The body is for the soul an outer revelation of his deep inner spirit and has the purpose of turning the intelligence and the free will of the soul inside out, limit it, and only from then on search and find the inner limitlessness of the intelligence, of the will and its true power, and by that, as an infinite glorified and completely independent individual to become one with the inner spirit, which is the only thing that really exists in the human being.

1.3 The two poles

The very strongest giant without a very firm opposing support, which we will call a counter-power or a counter-pole, is not able to do anything. The same relationship extends also, even if are going into the endless greatness, to the very highest divine being!

If the very freest, wisest and all-powerful Spirit of God had not given Himself, since the beginning, a counter-pole, it would never have been possible for Him, as a pure positive God, to call suns, worlds and all the countless many beings into existence.

But what does this counter-pole look like and what does it consist of? Is it a very foreign thing to the positive, free pole of divine life and power, or in a certain respect just the same? Is it a lord of itself, or does it depends in all its parts only from the positive pole of divine power?

The whole creation and everything that we can ever perceive with our senses are fixed thoughts, ideas and expressions of God, which are inherently alive and free. They are also responsible for their judgment and thus for their death, from which however they can free itself and become quite one with their spirit, which strives through its free will for the purely spiritual life, according to the laws of God, to be transformed into the free, eternal life as self-active and independent from its old death.

If the activity is a spiritual one leading to God, the love will also tend towards the spiritual and thus the Spirit also become active, and this activity is a good one and its consequences are the blessings from the heaven of life.

If a soul is enriched with things which are not serving love, his absence of love will turn him completely to matter and soon will become active in order to collect even more material treasures and through them it will spread more unpleasantness for the body. In this way, the soul is almost completely transformed into matter, as the counter-pole of the freest divine spirit. The necessary consequence of this is judgment in and through itself, the curse of life into death and in a certain way the unavoidable death itself. And who is guilty then, but the person himself, who has done this out of his mind, desires and actions!

In the first (positive) pole there is life, activity and freedom, in the second (negative) pole there is death, lethargy and judgment; and behold, this is what hell, Satan and the devils consist of – thus a corresponding description of what I have now described as the counter-pole!

Remember this! Wherever you speak to people, investigate whether they know something about the soul in themselves and about the eternal life of it! If they begin to shrug their shoulders in a certain way and say: "Yes, we have heard about it many times, but our daily experience teaches us that there is very little or no truth in it!"– Then you can come to the certain conclusion that these souls of such people have been almost completely consumed by matter and are all in judgment.

It will cost much to release them from their judgment and their counter-pole prison – already very difficult on this side and on the other side even more difficult, although not quite impossible. But for that a very long decline into their own judgment and death will be necessary, until the little spiritual part of the soul has quite consumed the own often global matter in itself and finally is forced by hunger to feel a great longing for a spiritual food. That will happen, but only after a length of time which is unthinkable for most of us.

Even God, if He had not given Himself out of Himself the counter-pole which is endlessly too great for our comprehension, would not have been able to call forth from Himself and set up any creation as existent materially, because the great counter-pole is the material creation itself.

And because it is what and how it is, it is also good in God's eyes (it is only evil in man's eyes, in its effect, because these have the designation in the soul and in part also in the flesh) as a being woken from death for eternity with the pure, positive spirit from God to unite with God, without thereby ever giving up its most absolute freedom and independence.

1.4 About Jesus Christ

Adam, as first human being on this Earth – that means as a human being with full spiritual freedom – was created to build a form from which matter could be led back to a free spiritual life. Most of all, to achieve this overcoming of matter itself, by free will, a condition had to be created, which express the overcoming of all the lower characteristics, like worldly lusts, wrong desires and tendencies, in order to make a free ascension to the purest spiritual life possible.

It has been said often enough that the human soul consists of very small parts, that develop to ever higher levels of consciousness to finally reach that form again in man and which cannot develop any further as an earthly form, except for what the form of the soul is concerned. So there are two principles in man: the peak of the material life, as the highest developed self consciousness being, and the beginning of a soul life, in the highest attainable perfection of nature, the human form. Therefore, on this knife edge of earthly life, man cannot ignore the awareness that he lives in him– for he himself is proof of that – while he still has no idea that he came at the doorstep of a spiritual life, which has now its beginning in the human form. In other words, after he went through many changes of physical forms – with the purpose to reach the human shape – this human shape, once achieved in its general form, does not change anymore. However, it is now that the soul begins to change, with the purpose to come ever closer to the Spirit of God Himself, and so to enter in communion with Him.

What can happen if this transition is not achieved, because here matter and spirit stand sharply against each other? They can both refine one another more and more, but – since they are polarities – they can never completely touch each other. Anyhow, a way must be shown here, a bridge built over which it is possible for matter to come to the spirit. And that bridge must be an example that everyone is able to follow. If someone would not walk on it, then it would become impossible to leave matter and come into a free, spiritual life.

So the Deity Himself – who pushed His created beings to walk the way of matter (out of love, to save them) till they reached the border from where the way of the spirit is possible – had to strive to draw them to Himself and bring them in this way into the relationship of father-child. Adam had to build that bridge in himself, and it was actually very easy for him, since the attractions of matter were very weak, compared to now. He only had to overcome himself – obedience – then the bridge would have been built and the spiritual life could have awakened and blossomed in him, because for man, who is for the rest free of every sin, obedience to God is the only mean to test him. It is only after disobedience that automatically all other offences follow, as everyone can easily notice with children. Now, Adam fell, and with that a withdrawal in matter had taken place – this means in that polarity – which can distance itself from God equally as far as it can ascend to God Himself, to ever greater bliss.

But with this fall, sin came into the world, because God never creates a work to destroy it again but continues to follow the way that was once taken and tries as it were to correct it, because divine wisdom takes the consequences of a failure into account beforehand. And when it comes to creating free beings – not machines – then the way of self-development in man is truly the only way to it. However, when the human race divided into nations, a succession of all sins occurred, consisting of a long series, leading to an ever deeper fall, because in its beginning – disobedience – was simply inhered. This means: if Adam had not been disobedient, also none of his descendants could have been disobedient, because then he would have destroyed the germ in himself that could not be inherited anymore. However, in this manner he fertilized the germ, and it grew in his descendants to become a tree that hardly allows the light of the sun to shine through its dense roof of leaves.

Now, often very strong souls have tried to break through this roof of leaves, to let the sun shine through it, and they succeeded partially, therefore mankind possesses very ancient religions. But those strong souls did not succeed to reach the core of the tree and break its crown to such extent that this mighty tree had to die. And they did not succeed because they themselves were not without guilt in their earthly life, since they first tasted the world before they felt thirsty for the truth and knowledge of God. The world tasted nasty to them, and only after that did they seek something better.

The old Indian religions are the oldest that we know today, because the old Egyptian religion in its true teaching was the oldest, but its knowledge has been lost. All those teachers were such strong souls. They broke through the roof of leaves for themselves, showing the way, and they described and declared what is true and real. Nevertheless, they could not write otherwise than for their time by which many things have become invalid now, which is easy to understand, considering the circumstances.

Before the encasing in the flesh as Jesus Christ, God was presented as impersonal by the true religion. This is why nobody could come to see Him, but only feel His Being, who could of course only show Himself as Light, because God Himself is pure light that sends out His rays. But when there is light, it is everywhere. It streams through everything and awakens everything to life. However, the impersonality of God necessitates not one point from where the rays are shining, like from a sun, but a sea of light in which there is no concentration. So, those who spiritually penetrated to the divine Being could not be aware of the Divine Being in any other way than as a life in the light – floating and resting in the light, uniting with the light without any desire.

Now, after Jesus became Christ, the personification of God, experiencing the deity was very different for those who came near Him – it was simply the drawing near of one person to another. Therefore, the old seers are right, but the newer ones, who lived after Christ, are also right.

After the fall of Lucifer, when the material world came into existence, the spiritual sun was created as the seat of the deity. But despite everything, it was not to be understood as a concentration existing in itself. The light in the spiritual world was everywhere, but to the physical man – as long as his soul was bound to that body – this spiritual sun did not become visible before Christ earthly life as Jesus. The fact that it became visible was a crowning of the faith of the spirit-beings, for it was only visible to them – but now also to the person who believes in God as soon as his spiritual eye is opened, because the Man Jesus can reveal His whole Kingdom at any moment to all who follow Him.

But the question remains: why can we find the same basic features in the old religions?

If it were not so, it would be surprising to the one who has understood these revelations, for if these old religions are forerunners of the teaching of the Son of Man and Son of God, then they also must contain the main features of the latter. They cannot contain things that are different.

If the old Egyptian religion would be entirely known in its oldest basic features – these only survived hazily in the present time by the later cult of the gods – then one would say: the Christian religion is derived from the old Egyptian religion. This is how strongly they look alike, especially if one would know the original meaning of the characteristics of Osiris, Isis and Horus.

However, to what extent did Jesus Christ succeed to break the tree of sins, and not to only break through the roof of leaves?

In the first place, everyone should clearly understand what it means "to sin". Many will soon be ready with the answer and say: sin is everything that is against God's will. Although this is true, but what is God's will actually, and how can man recognize it, if he does not even believe in God and even less recognize His will?

From this point of view, we can say: no one can sin against God, before one came to know Him. No one can be offended when a blind man claims that there is no light, only because he does not see it, and even less will God pressure the one who does not know Him, because of his foolishness. However, a blind man can offend his neighbor or someone else when he resists him in one way or another – even though he does not see him but he can hear and feel him and he is able to receive and enjoy his direct good deeds. He can sin against his love, for despite his blindness he cannot deny that the person exists.

This is also the case with someone who is spiritually blind. He certainly can sin against the commandment of neighborly love, even if he does not know God. Neighborly love is the way to the love for God – this has often been explained.

Now, since Jesus fulfilled this commandment down to the smallest detail – and this since his youth – the love of God grew in him so that he finally was absorbed by it. Sin had no power over him for he strove to go from the initial visible way of neighborly love, which was apparent through outer works, to the inner invisible way in the love of God.

God gave a commandment to Adam: unconditional obedience. He despised it and fell. Out of love for God, Jesus followed this commandment: not to do anything without the will of the Father, and through this he became the shining example to follow. So, he achieved in himself the level that Adam did not achieve, and in this manner he reconciled in himself with the deity.

Wisdom gave the commandment. The will, the power, produce its fulfillment. The love found the way in Jesus to fulfill the conditions that were necessary to bring back the former state of happiness for all created beings. Salvation lays in the fact that this way, which leads directly to God, is now opened and that this way was fulfilled by the Son of Man, Jesus, who became by that the Son of God, Christ. The death of Jesus is the sealing of the unconditional obedience. Even though it was not necessary for him, but since mankind, with its unlimited free will and by the influence of Lucifer demanded it, Jesus submitted himself also to this demand and died, physically.

Falling from one sin into another brings about an ever greater hardness of the soul. One speaks of stony hearts to describe this condition. How far this can go cannot be overseen. Matter, the outer lust, keeps growing, and naturally the awareness of any spirit-soul essential core becomes lost more and more. This hardening leads finally to an animal condition which only knows preservation and procreation, without inner spiritual freedom. Only a pure spiritual teaching can bring salvation from such condition and will lead to a moral awareness of human dignity; this teaching was briefly given, and could not be misunderstood in its greatest possible clearness. Acting upon it will break the chains of matter, will release the bonds of worldly lust for pleasure, and will finally lead the material wishes and desires to a condition of pure awareness as knowing evil, but no more doing evil, because this selfishness will melt down more and more. The more the selfishness will fade away, the more the shackles of matter will loosen (soften) and they will finally be no more felt as shackles.

So, the tree of sin was and could only be broken by Christ, because in himself he enclosed the Spirit of God, who already gave the commandment to Adam, which the latter did not obey.

Now, one will say: "But where is the proof that this is so, and that the former teachers did not accomplish the same? For what has been said here is hidden to the human eye. It is an inner process about which no one besides Jesus can report, while the outer process, the appearance of a great teacher, his life, his good teachings and also his death, happened many times. Now, how can the tree of sins be really broken by Jesus, and before him they only broke through the roof of leaves? This can hardly be noticed from the outer result in the world, because sin is flourishing in the present time as never before, and mankind cannot recognize the signs, except the outer ones."

Yes, this seems to be so at first sight, but when we look closer, it does not. All those who will go the inner way will soon realize what it is truly like. The outer appearance means nothing at all, for it is a hollow note. The one who does not want to go the inner way cannot be convinced or given an image of that way, just as little as it is impossible to give a blind person a notion of colors. Here the result decides. The way is there. Walk on it, and then make your own conclusion.

No one can come to the Father without meeting Christ first, and without faith in Christ no sage has ever felt the almighty Being of God as the very first Source of all love, who can make Himself personal. Only in Christ the impersonal becomes personal, and the union of these two in the human form of Jesus makes it possible for the creature to draw near to the Creator. The rising of matter into the Spirit, the leading back of the sequence of sins, that were committed upwards, beyond the wall that separates matter and spirit, as poles that cannot touch each other – are possible because the unity of these poles represented by the bridge which is the life of Jesus Christ.

Now, the question arises: before the death of the Son of Man, how far actually could the deceased souls go?

They could of course come to insight and also to inner bliss, this according to how they followed the teaching of the many earlier teachers, but they could of course not reach the point of viewing and interacting with the personified deity.

This happened in history for the first time when the body of Jesus was lying in the grave. There lay the purely earthly body, while the soul with the indwelling Spirit of God passed over and there showed Himself to all as the One whom He is and was.

With this manifestation in the spirit world, began the building and populating of the New Jerusalem, as the City of God, which will continue to exist forever.

1.5 *The Creation*

Moses, with his history of Creation, with his most fitting imagery, truthfully and in order with the eternal wisdom, he described the corresponding origin and onward development of all things, from their primordial beginning to their most supreme perfection.

Who does not interpret Moses in this way had better not read him at all; for reading and understanding him literally in distorted fashion, with just some modest thinking about it. In this manner, one will get completely crazy, becoming incensed with Moses" illogical foolishness and ultimately also about the wanton foolishness of all who, with sword and fire, impose upon mankind such illogical and most foolish doctrine, purportedly even inspired by God's Spirit, regardless of it seeming crudest foolishness even to themselves.

Who reads Moses with the foregoing and correct interpretation, shall find Moses a most true prophet of not only the most all-embracing wisdom, but also most profoundly saturated with God's Spirit, paired with the firmest will to impart to all mankind a knowledge of profoundest depth about God and all created things, in the way that he himself received it in his gigantic spirit from the Spirit of God Himself.

Thus, the suns originated for themselves, the planets for themselves, and also for their general interconnection. As such, man originated in the narrowest sense for himself, because the whole of Creation, in all its generalness, completely resembles and corresponds with a human, and because each individual of the whole Creation, spiritual and material, from the largest to the smallest, also corresponds and must corresponds with a human, because the human being is the actual reason and final goal of the whole of creation. He is the final product to be won by all the efforts of God.

And since man is that which God desired him to be and also achieved through all the pre-creations to which you stand here as incontrovertible testimony, everything in the heavens as well as the celestial spheres also corresponds to man, as Moses also indicated in his history of creation, and as also other tutors of mankind have done, although in a more veiled fashion.

Moses' Creation story, when applied literally to the natural world, would be the most obvious crassest nonsense for any man, moderately familiar with nature's ways and therefore having to declare the good Moses as a first class fool.

But he who takes the further course of Moses' books somewhat more seriously, must discern that Moses, with his language of correspondence, concerns only first man's primeval development upon Earth, and hence not at all the story of the Earth's and Heaven' creation, with all the creatures upon and in the Earth.

When Moses says: "In the beginning God created Heaven and Earth" then Moses does not by any means want this to be understood as applying to the visible sky and the visible, material Earth; for as a true sage he had in his lucid mind the fullest inner truth always. But this deeper wisdom he clothed in corresponding images, just as for a testimony he had to veil his shining face threefold before the people.

By Heaven is meant that God has placed the intelligence ability outside of His most eternal, spiritually most purified centre, as it were out of Himself. This is akin to a mirror, which has the ability to reflect external objects in it. However, in the deepest night and hence complete absence of light, the mirror obviously becomes a completely useless item.

Hence Moses, straight after the externalization of heaven, or the intelligence ability outside of God's life-centre, speaks of a so-to-say simultaneous creation of the Earth. Who and what is this Earth? By "Earth" Moses meant only the assimilative and attraction abilities of the externalized intelligences, which is almost the same what the worldly-wise Egyptians and Greeks called "association of ideas", where out of related concepts and ideas ultimately a truth-filled reality has to emerge.

If however the relatedness and mutual attraction was already incorporated within the intelligence abilities externalized by God, then the third conclusion automatically follows, that the kindred attracted and seized each other in actuality; for this deeply spiritual process, Moses could not have chosen a more appropriate image, than that of the material Earth, which in actuality is nothing else but a conglomerate of many related substantial particles, with the ability to attract one another.

"Darkness was upon the face of the deep!" Did Moses really want to indicate the lightlessness upon the newly created Earth? I say unto you that not even in his very first most foolish beginnings would the wise Moses have dreamt of such! For Moses was deeply initiated into the world of nature, and well initiated into the deepest Egyptian wisdom and science, to know that the Earth, an offspring of the Central sun, is at least a billion times a billion Earth years younger than the mother sun, and could not have been in darkness at earth's coming into being. Therewith, Moses rather indicating, again through imagery, that the abilities of intelligence and attracting relationship of the intelligence was not yet endorsed by any kind of cognition, understanding or self-consciousness, all of which being identical with the concept of "light"; but that it must result in the contrary, until they seize each other, then pressurizing and rubbing each other and, as it were fighting each other.

Have you ever noticed what takes place when stones or wood are vigorously rubbed against each other? Behold fire and light emerge! And behold, this is the light that Moses talk about that it come into being in the beginning.

What is meant by light we now know; but before that it also says that the Earth was desolate and void! That's a certainty, because with merely the capacity for being filled or even a perceived need for being filled, no vessel has yet been filled. For as long as there are no contents the vessel is desolate and void.

"The Earth was formless and empty". Such was also the case with the primordial creation. There were indeed a countless number of thoughts and ideas placed throughout all spaces of infinity by God's almighty will of His love and wisdom which thoughts and ideas we previously referred to as the individual, mirror-like abilities of intelligence, and that because each individual thought is as it were a reflection within the head of that which is constantly produced by the always active heart in itself.

Just as a thought or idea in itself is like an empty vessel, or a mirror in a dark cellar, just so was at the beginning the entire association of ideas, still desolate and void. However, as there is yet no activity of the intelligence abilities among them, but only the potential ability for being and action is present, it therefore follows, as already mentioned, that everything is still cold, and lightless.

"The Spirit of God was hovering over the waters." All these still inactive and motionless thoughts and ideas of divine wisdom are also extremely well compared to "water", in which also countless specific elements are mixed together, from which however, finally, all body-world takes its extreme diverse being.

But all the great thoughts and ideas developed within the wisdom of God, could nevertheless not have obtained reality, just as little as the ideas of some worldly sage, had he been lacking the means for their realization. Should any reality be capable of following the thoughts and ideas, then the relevant means and therewith a real activity of the thoughts and ideas acting upon them from within, which it must be be derived from some high power and authority.

If therefore some person has connected thoughts to ideas, wanting to see them realized, then he must, apart from loving the necessary materials, generate a mighty love towards them. But of such love his thoughts and ideas incubate as the chicks from a hen. Therewith the thoughts and resulting concepts become steadily more concrete ideas. And behold, such love is then that very Spirit of God within God Himself, which according to Moses moved upon the waters, which bespeaks nothing other than the formless and endless substance of God's thoughts and ideas.

Enlivened by this spirit the thoughts of God started to connect to become great ideas and one thought pushed another and one idea another. And behold, then according to divine order the "Let there be light! And there was light!" happened just like by itself. And as such also the natural great act of creation from the primordial beginning is explained as by itself and together with it finally also mainly the development process of the soul and spirit of a new born child until an old man and of the first human of the earth until our time and so on until the end of this world in everything!

Then there occurs a phrase in Moses that would make it appear as if only after the fiery love-action of the Spirit, resulting in light, does God begin to realize that the light is good; but this is not so by far, but only testimony to the eternal and endless wisdom of God, according to which this light is a truly free spirit life-light, generated out of itself by the action of God's thoughts and ideas, according to the order of wisdom, whereby in this manner the thoughts and ideas externalized by God, can continue to develop like by themselves according to their own intelligence as independent beings, naturally under the unavoidable constant influence of God. That is to be understood by this Moses" supplement, and not that God only after the creation gained the implicit insight that the light was something good!

Moses said: "And God divided the light from the darkness; and God called the light day, and the darkness He called night".

Firstly, one has to understand the metaphors as following: the independent life as the day, and death as the night; or freedom for day and judgment for night; or independence for day and bondage for night. Or, self-conscious love-life of the divine Spirit within the new creature, for day, and the as yet non-animated thou thoughts and ideas of God, for night.

However, this kind of order you again shall find also in every plant, where you right up to the tendril of the fruit find nothing but night and gnawing death, where the spirit of God still hovers above the water of dark deep, for the sake of the pre-developmental stage of the life-carrying matter. Once the foundation sufficiently firms up for the wheat-stalk of creation to have its final ring tied underneath the ear, enabling the actual spirit-life as truly independent to begin seize, feel and to comprehend itself in lucid self-consciousness, there certainly is occurring a division or rather separation of the light from the darkness, a liberated life from life under judgment, or, actually an indestructible life from a destroyable judged life, which equals death, under the general all embracing concept "night".

And furthermore it is said: "and from evening and morning became the first day". What is here the evening and what the morning? The evening here is the state when the condition for the eventual reception of the love-life out of God begins to consolidate through the influence of the almighty will of God. Once this has consolidated, the function of "evening" is accomplished and the free and independent action towards the self- development begins. Just as we call the transition from night to day "morning", correspondingly was the transition from the preceding condition of a judged creature towards the free, independent one, named "morning". And behold, here Moses by no means committed a logical error, when he allowed the first and all subsequent days to arise from evening and from morning!

The reason why Moses lets arise six such days from evening and morning is because, by careful observation and study, he saw that everything goes precisely along the same divine order of six periods, from its primordial beginning to perfection as that what it is, just like the full-ripe wheat on the dead stalk.

From the casting of the seed into the soil to germination: day one. From there to the formation of the stalk and suction and protective foliage: day two. From there to the formation of the last ring: day three. From there, the formation and structuring of the pod-like vessels, akin to the bridal chambers for generation of the free, independent life, with which the flowering stage also is to be counted: day four. From there, the dropping of the flower, then the rise of the actual already life-carrying fruit and its free activity, although still tied to the preceding, un-free stages, from which a part of the sustenance for forming the skins is taken, although from there on the main nutrients are taken from the heavens of light and true life-heat, up to the full development of the fruit: day five. Finally, the complete separation of the fruit ripened in the hull, completely on its own and now already perfectly independent, in its fullest consolidation by the pure nourishment of the heavens, therewith sustaining itself for the freest, eternally indestructible life: day six.

On the seventh day rest takes over and this is the state of the now completed, full-ripest and for eternity existing life, consolidated from the previous states, equipped with the full godlikeness.

The story indeed can have been only the sequence of intelligent human development and not a mute created nature, which has remained constantly the same right up to this time, and shall also remain so till the end of all time.

Such is the case also with the Indian Books, in which first the creation of the pure spirits and later the fall of same is treated of, only then passing to the creation of the material world and the animals and finally mankind.

All this is to be taken only spiritually, and explained mainly in terms of man's moral development.

Whoever is guided by the spirit and is familiar with the correspondence between the material and spiritual world, to him it is then also possible to discern how the material world has gone forth from the spirit world, and how finally the suns and planets and all the creatures upon them came into being.

But that is not so easy, because it means to be fully awake in the spirit. For only the arch-primeval witness to all becoming and existence can light up yonder labyrinths for you, behind which no mortal eye has penetrated, till now.

However, beyond everything, the age of the human race, like it is today, still agrees with the calculations of Moses, you can be fully sure of.

There certainly was upon Earth, long before Adam, a genus of strong animals which resembled the subsequent human species, not in shape but much more in instinct-like, nevertheless very sharp intelligence,. Nowadays, the elephant is a similar specimen of that genus (although physically much more imperfect). These large animals populated the Earth many millions of years, and therefore were forerunners to man. Through the weight of these large animals, the Earth's stony ground first had to be softened and made fertile for the precious fruits and animals which came afterwards, until it became capable of bringing forth man's sensitive nature, in accordance with Gods plan of eternal divine order, as laid into pre-incarnate nature souls, already living freely within the Earth atmosphere. This large animal race had long since for the greater part already disappeared from the Earth, when the first man in his godly majesty greeted the wide Earth. Notwithstanding this, remnants of these pre-inhabitants shall still be found in all periods upon and in the Earth, although mankind shall not know what to make of them.

After the Earth's ground was fully prepared, only then a most powerful soul was called from its free atmospheric nature to form a body for itself from the richest loam, according to the arch-primordial form of God, indwelling the soul. And the first, most mature and powerful soul did so, as urged from within by divine power; and the first soul so-to-say entered a powerful body, well-organized by itself, enabling her to fully behold the entire material world and the many creatures that were before her.

The wise man nevertheless shall thereby be lead to the conclusion that the Earth is older than the short time indicated by Moses, for which reason Moses shall fall into disfavor for a time. But other wise man shall be awakened by God, through whom Moses shall then be set in his fullest light, and from thereon it shall not take long for the full kingdom of God to seize hold upon Earth, and death shall forever disappear from this renewed Earth. Before then however much trouble shall yet come over the Earth.

Yes, the Earth's soil shall indeed have to undergo multiple manuring with the blood and flesh of men yet, and only through such spiritual fertilizer, a period of physical immortality shall set in, like at the times of Adam the era has begun, when the soul was able to build herself from the fat clay humus a perfect body in its God-shape.

But for those men, fully re-born already during their physical, the mortal life shall never reign over this new epoch, and they will live as pure spirits and angels, and everything will be fully entrusted to their guidance. In contrast, people who in that time had not achieved spiritual perfection, will in this newest epoch of the earth still be placed on this earth, but under much depravation, and will have to put up with the much strenuous servicing, which they shall find very bitter to taste, because they shall only too well remember their formerly happy state. This epoch shall be a long-lasting one, until finally everything have been transcend to spiritual existence, in accordance with God's eternal plan. And behold such is the way of God's order of all things, all coming into existence and being!

From this you can see, that even the slightest thought which ever was thought by a person, either on this or on another earth, is impossible to ever get lost; and the spirits, from whose thoughts, words, ideas and actions such a new world has been formed by the will of God, are soon recognizing in their perfected state, that such a world is a result of their thoughts, ideas, words and actions, and are pleased to take over with a great feeling of bliss the guidance, management, development and full revitalization and purposefully inner organization of the world body itself and finally of all things and beings, which exists on a such a world body.

You now look at this Earth and see nothing than dead-seeming matter. I also see the dead-seeming forms of matter; but I see much more in it, what you can't see with your eyes. I see in it the banned spiritual things and beings and feel their aspirations, and see, how they continuously grow in the inner development and better and more focused shaping and evolvement of their purposefully forms, and again I see countless spirits and little spirits, who are incessantly active like the sand in a Roman hourglass. There is no talk of any rest, and by their incessant activity the entire purposefully formation of all and every life in nature is created.

1.6 Space and Time

God, Space and Eternity are again equal to the concepts of Father, Son and Holy Spirit. The Father is entirely Love and consequently an eternal striving for the most perfect existence by the power of the eternal will in that love. Space, or the Son, is wisdom, coming from that eternal striving of love, as an eternal resulting existence. Eternity, or the Spirit, as the endless initial power in the Father and the Son, is the working of and the accomplishment of the strivings of the love in the Son.

If space have started from one point that expanded in all directions unto infinity, then firstly it was as little as infinite as the great Cosmic Man. Secondly, the question arises out of itself: what was that which undoubtedly surrounded that point endlessly far in all imaginable directions, from which later the infinite space of creation expanded. Was it the ether without light, or was it the heathenish chaos, or was it a complete firm substance, or was it the air, or the water, or the fire?

If it was one of those named things, then how did that point in space have the power in itself to drive such endless large quantities of substances out of itself, endless times into the infinite? And where did those substances end up if the eternal endless space came from this original point? Then, there is no other possibility, except that they have to be outside of the endless space, just like in the beginning, when they were also outside of that point out of which the endless space would have come forth. However, if this could be somehow imaginable, then the space of creation would again be limited, and even if it would expand eternally farther and farther, then it still could never be infinite.

With this you can see that the space of creation was out of necessity eternally endless in all directions and can never have known a beginning. And since in God, space and eternity are identical, then God, who unites all these attributes in Himself, is also without beginning, for a beginning of God is quite as inconceivable as the beginning of the existence of the endless space and of the eternal time.

Still, one can see a certain hard rock, and one still is not able to climb over it. Look, this rock exists of the fact that one is imagining the endless and eternal space as dead in itself, and without any intelligent life. If one has such an idea of the dead endless and eternal space of creation, then he can indeed very difficult (or not at all!) understand how the infinite Spirit-God was able to find also in eternity His way in the eternal endless death as a perfect life.

Therefore, the opposite is true. Imagine that in there is not a single little point without life and without intelligence, and what is in your eyes dead and which seems to be completely without life, is not dead and without life, but only judged by God's almighty will.

However, if all heavenly bodies with their most diverse elements are nothing else and also cannot be anything else except ideas and thoughts of Himself, that are fixed by God's almighty will, then how can they be considered as dead and without any intelligence?

If God, who is identical with the endless space and its eternal time, is in Himself entirely the highest and most perfect Life, then how can that which wholly comes out of Him be dead, without life and without intelligence?

Consequently, that which exists and which seems to be dead in our eyes is only judged by God in this way and can return to the complete free life as soon as God will unloose the firm bands of His will of such a judged thing.

Since all this is so and can't be otherwise, you should, in order to really come to a true representation of God, completely ban from the endless space all that which is in relation to death, and imagine nothing else than life and once more life and nothing else than intelligence, and once more intelligence, for in the endless Being of God's intelligence and power no death can exist.

The average human being, who is gifted with an individual life-consciousness, considers the endless space of creation and the unknown countless things which it contains as dead and therefore without intelligence. This seems to be like that because one must acquire the full godlike life's independence. For that, by God's will, man is completely separated from the universal life-consciousness, with its endless and highest intelligence, so that the life- consciousness of man would find itself in it and by that, as if by the external revealed way, he also would develop and strengthen himself for its eternal independent existence.

As long as one tries to acquire his life's independence by himself, he hardly has any notion that he is completely surrounded by sheer life and the highest life's intelligence and is also – as far as his body is concerned – permeated by it.

However, when he is ready for it, according to God's revealed will, because his inner spirit has completely permeated him, then the whole person is in free contact with the highest life and its enlightened intelligence in the universal infinity of God, without losing his individuality and personality by that. Then he discovers no more a dead space or dead stones, but then for him everything becomes life and light and intelligence, aware of itself.

The soul of a human being is only separated by very thin "wall" from the universal life's intelligence, and in his natural condition this is sufficient for him to have no idea of what is and what happens close by. And he does not even understand 1,000 times a 1,000 part of what is happening before his eyes. All this is because of the very thin separating "wall" mentioned before, that exists between his inner space and the universal endless spatial life. If this separating wall would be totally impenetrable, what would such an enormously isolated soul still know of what is existing around him on all sides?

The fact that a soul – for reasons only known to God – is separated by a stronger and denser wall of separation from the universal supreme intelligent godly life, you very well can see with the mentally deficient. Such a soul is thus only capable of a very poor development or sometimes even not at all.

Souls of animals and plants however are not severely separated from the universal godly life and are therefore capable, by their inner feeling, to do what they are destined to do, according to their capacity and strength. Every animal knows the food that is good for him and knows where to find it. He has his weapons and knows how to use them without any practice.

So also, the spirit of a plant knows exactly that element in the water, in the air and in the earth that is beneficent for its specific individuality. The spirit of an oak will at no time draw the elements to itself that the cedar needs for its existence. Indeed, who tells a plant to draw only that element that is intended for it? Look, all this is the work of the highest and universal life's intelligence of space. From this, every plant and animal soul draws a special necessary intelligence and is further active according to its nature.

But if this is so – something that every person can always clearly see from its experience – then it is obvious that the endless space and everything that it contains is life and a supreme intelligence. But the human soul (as the highest empowered mixture of mineral, plant and animal souls) has no memory of his former forms of existence, because the specific soul elements do not have a strictly separated intelligence, but for the benefit of their kind only a kind of intelligence that was taken from the universal godly life in space. Although in a human soul all the countless specific former parts of intelligence were united with each other, and this leads to the fact that the human soul can certainly recognize all things out of himself and can evaluate them intelligently, but a specific remembrance of the former levels of existence is not possible, because in the human soul there was only one human being that came into existence from the endless many separated souls.

However, when man is completely permeated with the Spirit of life and light, he will perceive such an order in himself, namely that everything exists out of the Father and that His Son (Christ) is everything in everything.

1.7 *Heaven and Earth*

Is it written: "In the beginning God created the Heaven and the Earth. And the Earth was without form, and void, and darkness was upon the face of the deep. And the Spirit of God moved upon the face of the waters. And God said: let there be light - and there was light! And God saw the light, that it was good. And God divided the light from the darkness. And God called the light Day, and the darkness He called Night. And the evening and the morning were the first day."

These are Moses" words. If one were to take these in their natural sense, one should have to at once see their ultimate absurdity.

What of a truth is the Heaven and Earth of which Moses says all was created in the beginning? In man, Heaven is the spiritual and Earth the natural. This still is void and without form. The waters are man deficient knowledge of all things, above which the Spirit of God moves indeed, but not yet within them.

Since God at all times however sees the terrible darkness in the material world-depth, God says: "Let there be light."

It begins thereupon to dawn within the nature, and God indeed sees how good is the light upon man's darkness, but it is man who do not want to recognize it. For this reason therefore a division takes place within man, day and night verily are separated, and through the day within, man then recognize the former night of his heart.

With man, his initial natural state is late evening and therefore night. Since God gives him light, such light is to him a veritable sunrise, and out of man's evening and sunrise verily come man's first day of life.

When a child is born, its soul finds itself in utter darkness and therefore night. The child nevertheless grows, receiving all kinds of instruction, gaining all sorts of insights with that. And this is comparable with evening.

Moses knew that only evening corresponds to man's terrestrial state. He knew that it was with man's worldly-intellectual education exactly as it is with the gradually waning light of natural evening. The greater is the pursuit of worldly things through men's intellect, the feebler is the pure divine light of love and spiritual life in their hearts. Therefore also Moses called such worldly light of men the evening.

Only when God through His mercy kindles a small light of life in the heart, does man begin to understand the nothingness of all that he had previously acquired through the intellect – his spiritual evening, whereupon he starts to gradually see how the treasures of his evening light are as transitory as this light itself!

The right light out of God however, kindled in the hearts of men is that morning which together with the preceding evening brings about the first true day within man.

God then divide the two lights, which bespeaks the two cognitions. The division itself however is the actual Heaven within man's heart, expressing itself in true and living faith and not ever in a void, intellectual musing.

For this reason, the one who has the mightiest and most undoubting faith is called "Peter" (like a rock), placed as a new divide between Heaven and Hell, and this fortification no powers of darkness shall overcome forever.

When this fortification is placed within man and his faith waxes ever mightier, then through such faith the nothingness of natural cognition becomes steadily more apparent. Natural cognition then moves to subordinate itself to the dominance of faith, and with that, out of man's evening and the steadily brightening morning, there arises the other and by far brighter day.

In this second day man already recognizes that, which alone must maintain itself as ultimate truth, forever and in proper order, is nevertheless still lacking within him. Man still continually blends the material with the purely spiritual, often spiritualizing nature too much and therefore seeing the material also with the spirit, therefore not yet being decidedly on the side of the right deed.

God then comes once again to help man along, provided man has done what he could from the strength loaned to him in this second day of his spiritual education. And this additional help consists in the provision of more abundant light, which then like the sun in spring, not just by greater light intensity but the warmth affected with this, starts to fertilize all the seeds laid in man's heart.

This warmth however is called love, and spiritually constitutes the soil within which the seed starts sprouting and thrusting out its roots.

After that, God said: "Let the waters be gathered together in certain separate places, so that the dry and firm land can be seen, from which alone the seeds can grow into living and enlivening fruit…and God called the dry land Earth, and the water, now gathered at certain places, the seas".

But the way it stands, this part has a purely spiritual sense and indicates how initially the individual and society at large develop in time, from their necessary original natural state to the gradually purer spiritual state of being.

Man therefore is being sorted out even in his natural state. The cognitions have their place – that is man's sea, and the love emerging from the cognitions as a soil capable of carrying fruit, washed all around by the totality of rightful cognitions, steadily renewed in its strength for the bringing forth of all kinds of select fruits ever more abundantly.

When man's cognitions therefore surround man from all sides and are progressively lit up and warmed by the love-flame which they had fed, then man correspondingly grows in strength and the capacity to act.

In this state God again comes to man –as love eternal speaks to man's love in his heart: "Let the Earth bring forth vegetation, the herb yielding seed, and the fruit tree yielding fruit after its kind, whose seed is in itself, upon the Earth."

Upon such Commandment from God in the heart, man gains a firm will, strength and confidence and goes into action.

His right cognitions take off like rain-laden clouds above the ordered sea and move over the dry land, moistening and fructifying it. And the Earth begins to turn green, bringing forth all kinds of grass and herbs with seed, and all kinds of fruit trees and bushes and seeds, yielding fruit, because that which the right intellect, translucent with heavenly wisdom now regards as fully good and true, that is also desired at once by the love in man's heart. Because just as the seed laid in the Earth soon sprouts, bringing forth manifold fruit, just so is the effect of the right cognitions if laid in the life-giving soil of the heart.

The seed however acts in the manner of awakening the love-force dormant in the soil, and this then gathers increasingly around the seed-grain, effecting the unfolding of the latter to growth, yielding fruit. In short, the right cognition moves to action only in the heart, and from the action all kinds of works emerge. And it is of this that, out of deep wisdom, Moses speaks in Genesis.

Man's former evening, raised to proper cognition through the light, thus leads to action, which must be followed by works. And this is the third day in the heart's development and that of the whole man in man, who is the spiritual man around whom everything revolves, on whose account Moses and all the prophets of God came to this world.

1.8 The Kingdom of Heaven

Everything we see now in the whole world represents the nature of the Kingdom of God. We should not think that the Kingdom of God is located in one or another place. The Kingdom of God is everywhere in the whole eternal infinity, and man who realizes this from the Spirit of the Lord, has the Kingdom of God in him, and he is everywhere in the Kingdom of God and in the full nature thereof, no matter where he is or stays or is active, or if he still is in his body, or in his pure soul as a spiritual being.

The Kingdom of Heaven is like a man who sowed good seed upon his ground. But while his servants slept, the owner's adversary came, casting sheer weeds among the wheat, which then sprang up with the wheat. Wherever the wheat came up with its fruit, there the weeds also came up.

When the servants saw this they came to the landlord and said "Lord, did you not cast prime wheat upon the field? Wherefrom came the weeds?"

The landlord said: "This has been done by my enemy!" And the servants replied: "Lord, shall we go and weed it out?" And the lord said: "Let it be, so that you would not trample and pull out the wheat with the weed. Let them both grow together till harvest. At harvest time I shall say to the cutters: "Gather up the tares into bundles first and remove them from the field to a place for burning, but afterwards gather the clean wheat into my barns. This is an appropriate parable of the Kingdom of Heaven.

The Kingdom of Heaven is like a mustard seed, which a man took and cast into his field. This seed of a truth is known to be the smallest among the seeds. But when it grows it is the biggest among the herbs, and finally a very fine tree, so that even the birds of the air come to build their nest among its branches."

The Kingdom of Heaven is also like a treasure hidden in a field, which a man found. And as it was too big and heavy for him to carry home, since he was still too far away, he went and buried it in the adjacent field at night, then went home happily, sold everything at home and bought the field at any price, for the treasure in the field was worth thousands of times more than what he paid for the field. And since the field was now his, he could safely take the treasure out of the field, since no one could dispute its ownership. Now he could easily move the treasure to his new house, which he had bought with the field, and no longer had to earn his living by the sweat of his brow, for he now enjoyed vast excess for life.

The Kingdom of Heaven is like a merchant who searched all the lands for good pearls. And he found a pearl of enormous value, inquiring of its price, and when told, he returned to his city, sold everything he had and then went and bought the big pearl, which in turn was of thousands-fold greater value than what he paid.

The Kingdom of Heaven yet again is like a net that is cast into the sea for catching fish, and when the net is full, the fishermen draw it to shore, whereupon they take out the good fish, placing them in a container, but the sick and foul they throw away.

Thus it shall also be at the end of the world. The angels shall go out and separate the wicked from the righteous and shall cast them into the furnace of their own wicked hearts, and there shall be great wailing and gnashing of the teeth, which is a true darkness of the evil soul, which shall constantly be in search but not find what will gratify its evil love."

The Kingdom of Heaven is exactly like a good soil in which the noblest grapes grow and ripen next to briers and thistles, and yet they both grow in one and the same good soil. The difference lays solely in their innate nature. The grapevine converts it to something good, the briers and thistles to something bad, useless and not enjoyable for any human.

Thus heaven also flows into the devil as it does into God's angels; but each of them makes different use of it.

Heaven is also like a fruit tree which bears good, sweet fruit. Now, various people come under its richly blessed branches who want to enjoy such fruits. Some of them are moderate and gratefully enjoy only as much as is good for them, where as others, who like the taste of the fruits begrudge it to others and do not want to leave anything on the tree, but eat it all until the last fruit has been consumed, so that the contented may not later find some more. After that they fall ill and have to die while the contented ones feel refreshed through the moderate consumption of the fruit. And yet, both parties had fruits from the same tree.

Thus heaven is also like a good wine which invigorates the moderate, but destroys and kills the immoderate, and so one and the same wine becomes heaven for one and real hell for the other, and yet it is drawn from one and the same barrel.

The actual true Kingdom of God for the true friends of God is everywhere, but nowhere for the enemies of God; because for these in turn everything is hell. Below and above, all is the same. Look neither up to the stars, for they are all earths like the one you tread, nor sink your eyes down to the earth, because it is under judgment, like your flesh, which must die and decay! But instead, seek diligently within your heart; there you shall find what you are seeking. For into every man's heart is cast the living seed, from which the eternal dawn of eternal life shall bloom.

The space within this earth floats, as well as the big sun, the moon and the countless stars, is limitless! One could, with the speed of thought, leave this earth and continue at such speed in a straight line – yet rushing along at such speed for eternities upon eternities. Then, after many eternities of flying at the speed of thought, one would yet come nowhere near to the end! Yet one would encounter everywhere creations of the rarest and most wonderful nature, filling and enlivening endless space, everywhere.

Nowhere there exists a separately created heaven, nor a separately created hell, for everything comes out from the heart of man; and thus, everyone prepares for himself either heaven or hell in his heart, depending on whether his actions are good or bad, and as he believes, wants and acts, he will live his believe, out of which his will was nourished and passed into action.

After the death of your body, through your heart you will step into the infinite space of God, and according to the state of your heart you will encounter it as either heaven or hell!

Let everyone examine the inclinations of his heart, and he will easily discover what kind of spirit prevails in his heart. If his inclinations draw the heart and its love towards the world and he feels within him a longing to become great and respected in the world, if the heart is inclined to become proud and feels discomfort with poor mankind and has the urge within to dominate others, the seed of hell is already lying in the heart and, if not overcome and nipped in the bud, will obviously prepare for such a person nothing but hell after the death of his body.

However, if a man's heart is full of humility and he feels happy to be the least among men, to serve all and disregard his own self because of his love for his brothers and sisters; if he willingly obeys his superiors in all things for the benefit of his brothers and love God above all, then in his heart the heavenly seed grows to a true and eternally living heaven. And this man, who thus has already all heaven in abundance in his heart, which is filled with true faith, the purest hope and love, can after the death of his body not possibly get anywhere else but to the Kingdom of God, which he has already carried in his heart in all its abundance for a long time.

For the one who seriously wants it, every effort and work is a soft yoke and a light burden, but when you will avoid the trouble, then with that you will not attain the desired goal as it should be. And the right trouble and effort are now the force, which every person should have in the Kingdom of God, in order to acquire it completely.

The one who want to acquire it in full earnest, will also do not avoid any trouble and any sacrifice, and God yoke seems to be for that one very soft and His burden that is laid upon that one very light and little.

And as it is now in these days and in this time, so it will be in the coming times with the worldly people, because on this Earth there will never be a complete lack of world-loving people, and for them His yoke will not seem to be soft and His burden will not seem to be light. And in their last days of their earthly life, with the prospect of the long night which lays before them, they will finally intend to acquire the Kingdom of God, they will have to knock on the doors, in order to receive a little bit of bread (only from the lowest Heavens!), for the satiation of the life of their soul.

Therefore, he who will do much for His sake and perform many actual sacrifices will also receive much from the Kingdom of God. But he who, just like the nightly traveler at the end of his trip through this world, will seriously start to knock at His door and to ask for help, will not be rejected indeed, but he will only receive little, because he only troubled himself little to acquire the Kingdom of God and he only started to search for it when he was forced by the extreme need.

Such a person has searched for the Kingdom of God with very little force and it is easy to understand that such a person cannot expect a great deal of the Kingdom of God. For with the same measure with which someone uses here, it will be measured in the Kingdom of God.

Thus, he who uses great force in order to win the Kingdom of God, will already receive great might and power here on Earth, but he who uses little force in order to win the Kingdom of God, will also receive little might and power here and in the beyond, and will never reach those who in His eyes, already here, on this Earth, have become great and mighty.

Seek above all to develop and to strengthen your life-consciousness according to Christ's teaching. Feel the need of the poor and relieve it according to your strength and wealth, comfort those who are sad, clothe those who are naked, give food to those who are hungry, and drink to those who are thirsty, help those who are sick where you can, free the prisoners and proclaim His gospel to the poor of spirit. This will exalt your feeling, your mind into the Heavens, and on this true path of life your soul will soon without difficulty become one with the spirit from God and will by that also share in His wisdom and might. And this will certainly be more valuable than to know much in the world, while being furthermore an insensitive human being towards fellowmen, and the true life in the spirit.

The spirit is the only true living thing in man, is pure love and most gentle and is an eternal supremely well disposed feeling of that love. Thus, he who will make effort to ever more absorb this love of the spirit into his selfish soul, becoming therein also more and more strong, more powerful, more courageous and more compliant, will help by that the full union of the spirit with the soul. And if the soul becomes then pure love and wisdom, then such a soul is also entirely one with his spirit and is therefore in the most living possession of all wonderful capabilities of life and existence of his spirit. And that is then certainly more valuable than having attended all the schools of the worldly scientists on Earth, but remaining by that a severe and insensible human being.

Therefore, refrain from spending all your time to research for the many circumstances of things and their phenomena, causes and consequences in the world, for this will bring the soul not even in 100 years even 1 millimeter closer to his true goal of life, because by that he cannot come to a true inner knowledge, but only to an external knowledge. Which most of the time is a blind guess, from which an ordered and coherent knowledge and insight can never arise! Because of that, the soul will find himself in a continuous anxious searching, which will produce no real salvation for life.

1.9 *Seven divine attributes*

The Seven Great Spirits (divine attributes) are the very thoughts of God and they are actually the primordial ideas arising from Him. The mystical number 7 means the perfect original divine and God-resemblance in every thought originating from Him and in every idea which He placed outside Himself.

The first in God is Love. It can be found in all created things, since without it nothing is possible. This idea is also called the Father, because all the others commence from it.

The second is Wisdom, as the light emanating from Love. This is the idea of the Son. This you can see in the form of every being; since the more a being is receptive to light, the more developed, defined and beautiful will be its form.

The third idea that arises out of Love and Wisdom is the effective Will of God. It is the Holy Spirit. Through it the beings thought of become reality, that they truly exist, otherwise all thoughts and ideas of God would be, what your hollow thoughts and ideas are, which are never put into action.

The fourth idea, which again originates from the first three, is called Order. Without order no being could have any permanent and stable form and therefore could also never reach a certain destiny. If you place an ox in the back of a plough, would you ever reach a goal with him?

The fifth Spirit of God is called the Earnestness. Without it no existing thing would be possible, since it is equal to the eternal truth in God and provide all beings with continuance, reproduction, prosperity and ultimately perfection. Without such spirit in God things would be very bad with all beings. They would all be like mirages, which appear to be something, as long as you can see them; but only too soon the conditions of production change, because earnestness is lacking, and the beautiful and wondrous images melt away into nothingness! They are well-ordered to look at, but since no earnestness prevails in the producing reason they are nothing more than highly transient images that can impossibly have a permanent existence.

Where the highest love, the highest wisdom, the almighty will, the most perfect order and the unchangeable firm earnestness are present, it is apparent that the highest Patience must also be present; since without it everything would become a rush and ultimately change into an inextricable chaos.

If a master builder builds a house, he cannot, alongside his other required characteristics, ignore patience; since if he lacks this he will never finish his house.

Patience is the mother of the eternal, unchanging compassion of God, and if this sixth spirit would not be in God, where and what would all the creatures be in relation to the almighty God?!

If in some way we transgress and therefore become apparently subject to the destructive curse of the divine love, wisdom, divine will, who's seriousness follows the preceding order, we bump into divine patience, which in time will and must bring everything into equilibrium, since without it all creatures irrespective how perfect, would be subject to the eternal judgment of destruction.

The divine Patience would be able to create, together with the preceding five spirits in God, one or even countless many people on the world bodies, and would also be able to maintain them; but then one or even countless many people would live forever in the heavy flesh, and the soul ultimately becoming free from the bonds of matter would forever be unthinkable. At the same time animals, plants and people would continuously reproduce and finally live in such large numbers on a space limited world body so close and crowded together, that one could not get out of the way of the other. All this will not happen if a world body under the rule of the infinitive divine patience would sufficiently mature, to carry and feed plants, animals and people. Yes, the creation of a material world, given the already known six spirits, would be infinitively slow, and it would be very doubtful if ever a material world would come into being.

But patience is, as already said, the mother of Compassion, and as such is the seventh Spirit in God, which we also can call it divine mercy. This makes everything right. It puts in order all the preceding spirits and causes the timely maturity of a world as well as all the creatures on it. For everything a certain time period is set, and the matured spirits can therefore soon and easily reach full redemption and enter into their eternal freedom and fullest independent life.

This seventh Spirits of God caused also that the Son of God himself came into the flesh, to redeem within the shortest possible time all the imprisoned spirits from the hard bondages of a necessary judgment of matter. Therefore also this undertaking – the redemption – the re-creation of all heavens and all worlds, can be called the biggest undertaking of God, since herein all seven Spirits of God in complete equilibrium collaborated.

This 7th Spirit in God, Compassion, as explained to you just know is active within the other six spirits, so that all thoughts and ideas of God could became reality, and he acts in a mighty way and the result of that is precisely the most perfect redemption.

1.10 The War between Heaven and Earth

Just as the 7 spirits, or special attributes of God, continuously battle with each other, so that one always challenges the other to become active, in the same way you can easily recognize the same battle to a more or lesser degree in all creatures of God.

Love on its own is blind, and its aspiration is to attract everything towards itself. But in this aspiration it ignites, and it becomes light and as such cognition and recognition is added to love. The light fights against the single aspiration of pure love and brings Wisdom and consideration to love. But at the same time, this war awakens the Will as the active arm of love and its light, who turns into action what the light has wisely put in order.

Then, out of cognition of love through its light and by the power of both, at the same time the very Order is generated, and fights against everything disorderly by the light and by the will of love, and you again find an eternal steady war of Heaven in Him as well as in all creatures.

Everything would be in good order, if one could guarantee some permanence, in what the four spirits so beautifully and orderly placed into action. But all the still so marvelous works of the first four spirits resemble the play of children, who with great enthusiasm and joy masterly put some things orderly into action, but shortly afterwards don't like the product anymore and destroy it with greater zeal than they had when creating. And verily, with the impermanence of all the creation, things would look quite badly.

To prevent this, resulting from the great pleasure for the perfect success of works, arises Earnestness from the four spirits, as a fifth spirit in God as well as in His creatures, and this spirit continuously fights against destruction and termination of the once created works.

In time, any work will show some deficiencies, and one will regret his hard labor and his earnestness during his zealous activity. One will want to destroy the work, hoping that by making new one will be more satisfied; but then, the sixth spirit rises against such idea, and this is – as already indicated – Patience.

Now, Patience on its own, united with the preceding spirits, would not carry out any special improvements to the work which has been done, but would nicely leave everything in place; and then comes the seventh spirit, namely Compassion, containing in itself mercy, gentleness, concern, diligence, charity and generosity. And the process to improve the work in a good way will start again, so that deficiencies of any importance are no longer present. This is once more a battle or a war in man as well as in God and in angels!

In God and in angels this war is always of such a nature, that one spirit continuously and with all its strength and power supports the other, and therefore every spirit is completely present in all the other. Love is present in all the other six and in the same manner the wisdom in love as well as within the other five spirits and so forth, so that in each individual spirit all the others are also completely and fully active and continuously support each other, in the most beautiful harmony.

This should also be the case of the human being, but unfortunately it is not so. Only a few people exist who bring all the seven spirits in them to a full and equal activity and thereby become truly equal to God and angels. Many are turned away from it and worry very little about it and thereby do not at all recognize the true secret of life inside them. Such blind and half dead people cannot recognize the very reason of life in them, since they are only guided and ruled by one or the other of the seven spirits.

And so, one lives purely out of the spirit of love and does not pay attention to any of other spirits. What else is such a person other than a voracious predator, who never gets enough? Such persons are full of self-love, full of jealousy and full of miserliness and are stonehearted towards all their neighbors.

Again, others have an enlightened love and are as such also quite wise and can give their neighbors quite good teachings; but their will is weak and therefore they are not able to put anything to work.

Again, there are others, with whom the spirits of love, wisdom and will are very active; but they are very weak with the spirits of order and proper earnestness. Those type of people will be able to talk very clever and sometimes even quite wise and are able to put here and there a very few things to work; but a wise person will very soon notice there is no order and no coherence in their thoughts, speeches and works.

And again, there are people who have love, wisdom, will and order; but they lack the spirit of earnestness. Therefore, they are afraid and not able to provide their works with truthfulness, continuity and ownership.

Again, others are full of earnestness and courage, but the patience is lacking. Such people normally rush too much and often ruin with their impatient zeal more than make good. Without the right amount of patience there is nothing that last sufficient enough to make a difference. Who doesn't have the right amount of patience, speaks a certain death sentence over himself! Because one has to wait until the grapes are fully ripe, if one wants to have a good harvest!

Patience is therefore in each and everything a necessary spirit: first to control and to restrain the spirit, who often wants to go to infinity – since this spirit in conjunction with love, wisdom and will degenerates into the most severe form of arrogance, who as is generally known does not find any limits in man; and secondly, because patience is the mother of the spirit of compassion, which is the spirit who provides, by its backward action, to all preceding spirits, the divine-spiritual perfection and makes it possible for the soul in man to reach the true rebirth in the spirit.

Therefore, the Lord Himself laid it onto the hearts of all to love God and your neighbor, by saying: "Be merciful, as your

Father in heaven is merciful, and be meek and humble, just as I am, with my whole heart, meek and humble!"

The Lord instructed us all to develop especially compassion, since with this last spirit all preceding spirits are easily contained and trained. Therefore, one who develops and strengthens this last spirit, easily afterwards develops and strengthens the preceding spirits and thereby certainly soonest reaches the divine perfection. Who starts his development with one or more of the preceding spirits, reaches with more difficulty (often just partial!) the complete and full perfection of life.

This is also the continuous fall of the angels, devils and men, as long as they haven`t developed, in their entirety being, the seventh spirit to the highest perfection.

1.11 Angels, Men and Devils

The first ideas of creation were placed in an isolated and independent existence by a positive "must", from the immutable will of the primordial Light. Therefore, as concerns the separation and forming of the limited existence, this was accomplished by this immutable principle called "must".

Now, the entity was there, in its inner being, to a certain degree, the deity itself or, which is the same, the primal essence of God, only separated from his First Cause, although conscious of it, but still bound in a limited form and restrained by an immutable "must". The entity did not relish this state, and his feeling of exaltation (felt because of the awareness over the inner primordial essence) came into a mighty conflict with her inevitable feeling of limitation and separation, created by this inflexible law called "must".

Since in the very first line of beings the inner conflict kept growing in intensity, the great fundamental law had to be tightened to hold these beings in a firm judgment, so a second fundamental low come to existence, called "should", which basically consisted in the manifestation of the universe as it is, with its solid globes. This second law 'should", effect the first division between the primordial beings. Some of them (the angels) accepted the judgment and took their roles in the newly formed universe. The rest have chosen to resist and became defiant, arrogant and disobedient to this mild law, no longer given with "you must", but only with "you should".

This behavior pushed these beings even further from the Light; therefore, a second judgment came to help them to recover their divine state of existence, and from this appeared which basically consisted in the so-called World of Man.

Among the remaining entities, some of them took this new chance and they became Men and they follow the necessary ways for developing themselves towards the divine life of their spirit in the human flesh. The rest, because they refused and they are still refusing to submit to this even milder "you should", a more severe and mightily sanctioned law was promptly effected.

Following this limitations, the divine primordial being appears in its own fullness, namely in the person of Christ. Thus the original grace returns once more, takes all the weaknesses of the limited existence upon Him, giving to all of the created being a new grace, a new life full of true light and showing them in this light and through His example the right way and the true purpose of their existence.

And now, also the limitations which had been created through the laws could be abolished and everybody could at any time free himself from the burden of the laws, if he exchanges his old nature for the new one, out of Christ.

That is the annunciation from the bosom of the Father and the living Gospel of God.

2 ABOUT MEN

God is the tree of life and we are its fruit. The fruit does appear to be smaller and less creative than the tree, but in its centre there lays a seed that is nourished and matured by the fruit. In the seed, however, there are again trees of the same kind, capable of bearing the same fruits again with living seeds, like the one they have gone forth from.

From this, one can easily see that the difference between Creator and created being is in a certain respect not as great as we imagine, for in the created being is the will of the Creator, which is certainly good and worthy. If this will, gone forth from the Creator and under the form endowed with an independent life, recognizes itself in its free isolation as what it fundamentally is and acts accordingly, then it is equal to its Creator and in its limited way fully that which the Creator is in His infinite way. If, however, the part-will, made independent by the Creator, does not recognize itself as what it is, it does not cease to be that, but is unable to reach the supreme goal, until it has recognized itself as what it fundamentally is.

2.1 *Evolution to the human form*

The Romans have a quite good proverb, which says more or less the following: *Longum iter per praecepta, brevis et efficax per exampla!* (Long is the way by teaching, short and effective by example!)

Haven't you noticed that in nature only one law exists for the growth of all plants and animals?! All plants grow and multiply from within; they draw their corresponding substances from the moisture of the earth, purified them by passing through thousand channels and small pipes, and finally nourish themselves.

Animals take their food basically from the same source – with the only difference that it is either by the organism of plants or in the already much more refined flesh of the lower level animal species, much more purified than in the original humus of the earth.

Man finally enjoy the already most refined and purest food, from the plant world as well as the animal world. Hay, grass and straw does not feed him anymore. From plants he uses mainly the noblest, honeysweet fruits. From animals he enjoys mainly only the recognized purest ones and is disgusted by the meat of completely impure animals.

But how many deviations, aberrations and detours exist with only the physical unfolding of the plant and animal world, and still each reaches its goal! It cannot go unnoticed to the observant eye of a researcher of things in the physical world, how always one thing serves the other and how one is present to lift and further animates the other.

Life must work itself through the different physical elements. First it is in the ether; it collects itself by seizing the same with the same, similar and related. Thereby it becomes heavier and at first sinks in itself, in its own centre, becomes heavier and heavier and becomes out of itself the already heavier and noticeable substance of life.

In the air it collects itself again as in the ether, from that clouds and fog are formed, which become water drops and fall in the form of rain, hail, snow and dew to the earth and in certain areas are remaining as a constant haziness and moisturized precipitation from the air.

The water, as a still subordinated, but already over ether and air standing element of life, must already start to serve the quite manifold and higher standing life condensation institutions. First it must soften the life in the coarse matter which has hardened as rocks and must also serve as reception and further transportation in itself, which assimilate into the element of the water: this is the first manner of serving.

Thereupon, it must give its spirits of life or so to speak soul-like substance particles to the plant. If the particles in the plant with time have developed more and more into certain intelligent forms, they will again be absorbed by the water and the hazy air, and the water must provide them with substances to become new and freer life forms. Therefore, the water still serves in its sphere, although, from it hourly myriads times myriads small-soul-life-intelligence-particles become free and more and more independent.

However, the plant life must again accept and provide several and already more complicated services. The services of the water are still very simple, while the services of plants are already very much involving the further promotion of life, as it is shown even by a very simple plant.

Even many times more and very significantly are the services to promote the soul-life itself in the very first and simplest animals. And so the serving becomes increasingly complicated in every higher standing life form.

Once the soul life has completely and entirely transformed into the human form, to serve is its first destination. There exist different physical services which are given to each human form as a "must"; with it there also exist a countless number of freer and an even greater number of most free morally services, which a person is given to execute. And if one has become a loyal servant in every aspect, one thereby has elevated oneself to the highest perfection of life. Now, this in fact takes place with a few people, who already from birth have been placed on a higher level; but with other people, who are so to speak still standing close to the line of animals, it doesn't happen too much on this earth, and their further development can only progress in the beyond, but always along the fundamental path of evolution of the capacity of serving.

2.2 *Body, Soul and Spirit*

The body is matter and consists of the coarsest primeval soul-substance which, through the might and wisdom of God's eternal Spirit, is forced into yonder organic form corresponding to the shape of the freer soul indwelling such physical body.

The soul indwelling such body initially is of course not much more pure than the body, because it derives also from the unclean, arch-primeval soul-substances. Actually, the body is for the unclean soul nothing more than a very wise and well-attuned purification machine.

Nevertheless, within the soul already resides the pure spark of spirit, with which she receives a proper self-consciousness and the divine order in the voice of conscience.

Besides that, the body is outwardly provided with all kinds of senses, being able to hear, see, feel, smell and taste, whereby the soul is diversely informed about the external world, good and true as well as bad and false.

Through the discernment of the indwelling spirit, she soon feels within herself what is good or bad; on the other hand, through the external bodily senses she obtains experience of good and bad, what is pleasing and what is painful, and other impressions, and on top of that, by the way of extrasensory revelation from within and from without, the soul is shown the path of divine order through the Word of God.

Thus equipped, the soul indeed is capable of free self-determination within the easily recognizable divine order, which of course cannot be otherwise, or the soul could not possibly obtain an enduring, self-contained free existence.

Every soul desiring to continue to exist must become capable of enduring existence and, as it were, develop her completely, through means put at her disposal. Otherwise, she will not be able to use a human body, which becomes entirely not conductive to the soul's further anymore, and the soul will have no choice but to continue its development in a much more uncomfortable "body", usually under very sad and painful circumstances.

The human body however, in the narrowest sense, is every person's hell, because it consists of particles still under deepest judgment and therefore capable of dying; the matter of all the worlds is hell in its broadest sense, into which man is placed through his body.

Hence, one who cares too much for his body is actually looking after its personal hell, feeding and fattening its judgment and death for its most personal demise.

The body indeed has to receive a certain degree of nourishment, in order to be constantly capable of serving the soul for its lofty life-purpose; but one who is too attached to the body, wrangling and working and bartering for it nearly all day and night, obviously is taking care after its hell and death.

When the body stimulates the soul into throwing itself headlong into hedonism, than this always stems from the many impure nature or matter spirits under judgment, which actually in effect make up the body itself. If the soul pays too much heed to the desires of the body, acting accordingly, then she unites with them and therewith descends into her very own hell and her very own death. In doing so, the soul commits a sin against the divine order within her.

If the soul persists therein with exquisite contentment, then her uncleanness rivals from her body, the most unclean and judged spirits continue therewith in sin and therewith hell and death. Notwithstanding her continued life in the world, like that of her body, she is as good as dead, feeling also the death within her and much fear. For whatever the soul is doing in its sin and hell, she nevertheless cannot find life, notwithstanding her love for it beyond all measure.

This is also the reason why many thousand times thousands of people know no more about the life of the soul after death than a stone by the roadside; and if anything is said to them about it, they only laugh or even turn wild, driving the sage out the door, telling him to preach such foolishness to wild boars!

And yet, every person by their thirtieth year should be as sufficiently mature for the fullest awareness of the soul's life after physical death of the body as flight is to the eagle in free air high above.

But how far removed from there are people who are only just beginning to ask about it! And how much further still those who wish to hear nothing about it, even holding such belief as foolishness not worth a laugh! Such people find themselves in fullest hell and death their whole earth-lives long!

A soul nonetheless may have already completely cleansed itself and yet be granted often a lengthy period of earth-time for cleansing of its still unclean body and the latter's spirits, and then the noble parts of the body attracts the soul's immortality and shortly after death awakens the coarsest particles of its being for fullest augmentation of the soul.

With such cleansed soul it can occasionally still happen, if the body asserts itself hedonistically, thus it enters into its own hell, so-to-speak entering into the lust of the body and its spirits. Such souls can no longer be made completely unclean, being unclean only for as long as indwelling the mire of her bodily spirits; but they are no longer able to tolerate it therein for much longer, returning soon into their completely pure state, whereupon they are again as pure as if they had never been unclean. Therewith they restored peace and order within their hell, being afterwards capable to move about and fortify themselves within the light of their spirit.

The soul lives herself either through a wrong direction into her flesh, or through a right direction into her spirit, which is always one with God, like the light of a sunray is one with the light of the sun.

When the soul lives gradually more and more into the flesh, so that finally become full flesh herself, then she is also overcome by the feeling of destruction, which is a property of the flesh; and this feeling is then the fear which finally makes men in all things absolutely incapable and weak!

It is however an entirely different matter with a soul who is living into her spirit! There the soul forever does not see any possible destruction! Its feeling is akin to the state of its eternally indestructible spirit; she can see and feel no more death, being one with its eternally live spirit, who is lord over all the visible natural world, with the result that all fear is far from the still incarnate soul; for where there is no death, there is no fear!

But there are parts of matter that shall never be part of a soul, and these consist in what is known as shell or encasement material, within which always some soul potency is enclosed, up to a certain development of independence. Once the special soul potency has achieved a certain maturity, it ruptures the encasement, immediately uniting with previously liberated similar spirits, or at least corresponding individual potencies, afterwards creating for herself some other husk from corresponding elements of the air, water and soil, thus immediately another shell as you can see tangibly with seeds of plants, trees and shrubs and notably as with eggs of insects, birds, marine animals and so on.

The encasement material is merely a fixation of willpower going forth from God's order, and as such containing no soul-intelligence, being only a necessary means for a soul-intelligence to, as if out of herself, in isolation and over time, actually developing into an independent being.

Wherefore, the world of matter is by up to two thirds soul and one third soulless hulls, as carrier of initially individual and gradually consolidating and finally fully mature and ripe soul-life. Therefore, the encasement material, or God's fixed will, is also a salvation institution, through which the individual, primeval fallen spirits can, along the established order, regain yonder perfect, independent liberty, although along a more extended path than the first period could have been.

However, time does not trouble or tire God, because He constantly keeps the achievement and realization of His great ideas before His all-seeing eyes. For God, a thousand years are as a day or a moment; so, planet like Earth can require an unspeakably great number of years for the release of its spirit, which is captive in its husk-material; and ultimately, that is to God as a fleeting moment.

There are indeed some worlds within infinite Creation-space that have already completed their service. But they nonetheless continue to endure as celestial spheres, continuing to do so as carriers of the new, free beings, although they now are much more pure and sound, and also unchanging in their structure; God's solid will corresponding to His wisdom, and eternally consistent order has to be unchanging, since no being could have a duration without such firmness.

Because even if the beings, after their spiritual perfection, possessed a completely free existence, as if completely independent of God, such independence could still not have any permanence if not fixed from eternity within His order, and as one with it. However, this fixation from eternity is in reality for all created beings the very thing providing them their constant duration and maintenance.

However, from this it arises like by itself that nothing which has ever been created by God in whatever form, can never cease to exist or be disposed of. It can change its form and progress from a lesser to a more perfect form, also in reverse, as we have seen such with the primeval created spirits; but nothing can ever be destroyed, once given existence by God, including the human Spirit.

But what is in fact the Spirit of a human being?

What one calls the human Spirit, or the Spirit out of God and actual life, is only a spark of divine light in the centre of the human soul. This spark must be nourished with spiritual food, which is the pure Word of God. Through this food, the spark becomes larger and more powerful in the soul, finally it even takes on the human form of the soul, and fills the soul once and for all; in the end, the spirit transforms the whole soul into divine light, and then, the soul itself becomes complete free life which recognizes itself as such in all profundity.

As long as man is a creature, he is temporal, transitory and cannot endure, because every man in his natural state is merely a suitable vessel within which a human spirit can develop, through God's constant participation.

Once the human body, which is the outer vessel, has reached the right degree of development, to which God has abundantly provided all essential parts and properties, He then awakens or rather develops the eternal human Spirit within man's heart, and this Spirit in its effect is what Moses presents in the fourth day of creation, taking about the two great lights which God put in the celestial firmament.

The purely divine or uncreated Spirit of God, placed permanently into the celestial firmament is the great Light. Man's Spirit however, which is almost equally to the great Light, is the smaller and lesser light, which (like the uncreated great Light) is placed in the same celestial firmament and transformed to a co-uncreated light, without losing any of its nature, but instead gaining endlessly in a fully spiritual sense. By itself man could never see God in His purest divine nature, and the purest uncreated Spirit of God conversely could not see the natural, because for Him nothing material-natural exists. But through the above mentioned complete conjunction of the uncreated Spirit with the human Spirit, the latter can now see God in His arch-spiritual purest being through the life that he received, and the Spirit of God can then see the natural through the Spirit of Man.

This is what Moses is saying when he is talking about the great light who is to rule the day and the lesser light the night: to determine out of all wisdom the basis for every appearance and all created things, therefore also determine the times, days and years. Which is to say: to recognize God's wisdom, love and grace in all phenomena.

The stars which Moses also mentions are the countless useful cognitions - every individual thing, which latter of course all flow from the main cognition, and are therefore placed in the same heavenly firmament, as the two main lights.

2.3 About spiritual development

Every human being, who really wants to know himself and God, must enter this extremely inconsiderable little chamber of life within his heart, by the ways of extreme humility and compliancy, and give back spiritually the life that was received from that. When a human being acts like that, he makes the little chamber of life bigger and illuminates it more and more. When that happens, the whole heart (and from the heart the whole human being) becomes enlightened and he knows himself, and by that also God. For only then he can become aware and he can see how the life from God enters this little chamber, gathers itself and develops itself to a free independent life.

Consequently, in this little chamber lives the human spirit, which is actually a Spirit out of God, and if the soul of the human being enters this little chamber by the right humility and compliancy – as the love of the true human being enters the eternal, uncreated love of God – then by that the soul unites with the eternal human spirit, and that is the rebirth of the soul. When the eternal Spirit out of God (the human spirit) unites with the uncreated Spirit of God this is the rebirth of the human spirit.

That certain extremely inconsiderable positive little chamber of life of the heart, the actual foundation of men's life, is also alone capable of the most clear and most true intelligence, and thus it is already within itself the light, the truth and the life.

Everything that you think in your brain first comes from the heart, for every small thought first must have a stimulant through which it is called forth as necessary. Only after the thought is animated and produced in the heart, in accordance with some need, does it rise to the mind for examination, so that the latter can set the bodily limbs into the corresponding movement, so that the inner thought may so to say become a word or deed; but for any man to think just in the head is a sheer impossibility. For a thought is a spiritual creation and can therefore not arise in other place than within man's spirit, which resides in the soul's heart and from this place animates the entire man. How any creation could develop from any ever so rare matter, since all matter, including man's brain, is nothing but pure matter and hence can never be a creator, but only a creation?!

Thus, with people whose love has not yet awakened, the thoughts, although forming in the heart as well - on account of the latter being still too material - are not discerned within the heart but only in the mind, where the thoughts of the heart, already more material, develops pictorially, amalgamating with the images which have imprinted themselves in the brain tablets from the outside world, through the body's sensors, becoming so to say material and bad in the soul's view and therefore having to be regarded as the necessarily evil basis for man's deeds.

Therefore, every person must be born again in the heart, and there in the spirit, or he cannot enter the kingdom of God!

But most of the human beings on this Earth are very inconsiderable, blind, dark, little, weak and powerless. But in the hidden inner kernel of their life they are the fundamental life point of the whole great Man of Creation, and they can also develop out of themselves very high abilities of life.

Thanks to such very high and godlike abilities of the people of this Earth namely: a well-articulated outer and inner language, the art of writing and arithmetic and still a lot more other things - they are also capable to understand the revealed Word out of God's mouth, for instance first in the external meaning of letters or images, and then in the true spiritual meaning, and finally in the deepest meaning of the heavenly life.

These abilities are something invaluably great and outstanding, just like the abilities of life and intelligence of the positive little chamber of life of the heart, which are the most perfect and most noble part of the whole human being.

The spirit of man, once awakened in a proper manner, discovers many secrets, and if fully awakened in the full light, he also discovers the great secret of life and recognizes God as the originator of all life. But it is the greatest art of living, to find and recognize oneself as such!

People live and think and want and become active according to their thinking and will; but they do not know what life is, how it thinks and how it wills and how it makes the limbs correspondingly active. The soul lives herself either through a wrong direction into her flesh or through a right direction into her spirit, which is always one with God, like the light is one with the sun. If such a soul lives into its flesh, which in itself is dead, by that the body receives a life from the soul, and the soul in everything becomes one with its flesh.

Hence man should concern himself as little as possible with the things of the world, so that his soul would become one with the spirit and not the flesh! For what does it profit a man to gain the entire world for his flesh but suffer exceeding harm in his soul? For all the world which we now see in its wide surrounding, with its passing glories shall pass like water-bubbles and also this sky with its stars in due course; but the spirit shall remain forever, together with every one of My words.

But it is inexpressibly hard to help people who have firmly settled into the world, for they see and plant their life into the vain things of the world, living in constant fear and being in the end utterly unapproachable along spiritual paths! However, if one approaches them along the natural and worldly path, then one not only benefits them nothing but only fosters their judgment and therewith death of their soul!

Who from the world-people wants to save his soul, must apply a great force onto him and must as much as possible start to live in abstinence with regard to worldly things. If he does so diligently and keenly he then shall save himself and enter into life; if not, then he cannot be helped in any way other than great sufferings in things of the world, so that he learns to despise the world and its glories, turning to God and beginning to search out the spirit within him, to gradually unite with it. The blessedness of the world is the death of the soul!

All those who will follow God and His words will reach the rebirth of the soul. So this is when the soul has become pervaded by the spirit, by which he is already capable in the body to penetrate in all higher wisdom of the Heavens and become lord, not only over himself but with that also lord over his environment, even over nature and its hidden powers. The means to reach that goal are called: Love for God and love for fellowman.

Such re-born people can and must also be very righteous people, such as there existed at all times and who possessed the highest completion of the soul, but therefore they had not necessarily reached the community with the personal active Spirit of God, which is the highest completion of the spirit.

This is not possible till the Deity is not personally visible. All righteous people, who reached the rebirth of the soul, would despite that still by far not see the God in person. That is why their teachings show that penetrating into the highest completion seems like ascension into infinity, because God Himself, as non-personal being, means infinity, in which the blowing of His power can spiritually be felt, but His person could not be accessible.

Only when there is an interaction with the infinite deity Himself, impersonal, all those who reached the completion of the soul (rebirth of the soul), will be also capable, by interacting with the deity in person, named Christ, to live in eternal community with Him, and reach the completion of the spirit (rebirth of the spirit).

All humans are very well able to reach the rebirth of the soul following the Word of God and therefore also they are very blessed and happy, but without reaching the highest and last level, the rebirth of the spirit. Many representatives of the Spirit of God descended to the Earth and show the way to the lost people, how they could come to peace and inner enlightenment. All who wanted to walk on the former ways in this manner can thus very well come to the rebirth of the soul, but not the rebirth of the spirit.

The latter is only possible by believing in Christ, to whom all power and glory of the Father is given, so that the people will become happy and highly blessed through the Son. The Son is the Gate – there is no other. If one wants to walk on the ways to Heaven without wanting to know the Son of God, one can reach a high degree of completeness, but will never come to clear, visible community with the Person of God.

The difference between the rebirth of the soul and the rebirth of the spirit is relevant only for the ones who are capable to know and to feel the difference between the spiritual and the physical man.

Firstly: How do we experience thinking and feeling? Is it outerly, or innerly? That means: can we only answer a question that is asked to us because we used previously learned knowledge from our teachers, or does our own inner self answer the question by reasoning?

One will say: "This can be both!" If man were only a machine, although provided with a self-conscious soul, he would only be able to think outerly. That means: to obtain knowledge by means of impressions in his memory, which were only acquired by what he learned – somewhat like one trains an animal (or a computer - editor's note). To reason could mean also that the soul asks questions to an inner principle that lives in man and which answers questions that are asked and which also lives in the soul as spirit that is perfect as such. That is why a real activity of questions and answers can take place in the inner of man.

One will say: "Yes, if the spirit is perfect, then how come that often such enormous foolish conclusions can come up? Does the spirit then not give always the right answer?"

The spirit does answer correctly, but since it is in man in the first place the life's principle of the soul, this one can, as she is self-conscious, also act according to his nature, like a mirror image. As a real mirror image cannot exist without the presence of an object which is exactly the same, so also the soul can only give his opinion freely when these come from the spirit as reflections. But, as a mirror image represents everything in reverse, this is also what happens here until them both seek to merge with one another.

Only that one, who has awakened the Spirit to such degree that the soul no more reflect earthly, reverse reactions, has reached the rebirth and stands in the full truth. It is of course not easy to break through those barriers, because the earthly adjusted soul is strongly attracted by the material-earthly body than by the spirit, which influence is only weak and of which he gladly accepts the activity as his own work, if he did not learn to see the difference.

To break through those barriers is our task, and the way to it we can find by our inner spirit and we need to let him speak. He is the only, one true teacher because it is connected with the universal Spirit of God and is a small image of it, and therefore he draws all truth only from Him.

Now, when the soul has made herself completely subordinate to the nature of her spirit and by that she has no more earthly wishes so that she solely strives to the spiritual and has therefore, as a self-conscious soul, passed into the spiritual, then this more completed person has reached a level that was indicated by the Indian sages as "Nirvana". This is a condition in which every will, based on fleshly, earthly tendencies, is destroyed and which eliminates the life in the flesh as material existence. This condition is possible in the material life and it has to be reached so the total peace will come into the heart of man.

However, in the Kingdom of God, there is still another rebirth, which is the one of the spirit, which will then consist of an inseparable community with God. There will be the highest bliss of the children in the house of the Father and joys which no human heart can ever suspect, because they are purely spiritual.

Most of all, one must strive to reach the rebirth of the soul, so that soul will learn to only look with the eye of the spirit and will know by that more and more about himself and his origin.

The final goal of the spiritual development is to become one with the all-filling, all-penetrating and all-working Spirit out of God. This spirit is residing in the innermost center of our soul, but it is isolated from the universal Spirit, because of too little love for God, which means to receive a much too little spiritual nourishment. For this reason, the spirit cannot expand itself in the soul and penetrate him and thus expand itself throughout the whole human being. This does not mean spatially, but in the sphere of the will, which is just as present in it as in God Himself, by whom it has been laid in the heart of the soul as an indestructible life-spark.

However, to expand the sphere of the will means the soul submits his own will completely to the recognized will of God and voluntarily allows to be ruled by it.

If this is the case, that the soul – as if from outside – allows himself to be penetrated in his innermost by the recognized and precisely followed will of God, then he awakens the Spirit out of God that is resting and slumbering in the innermost of the soul. It unites itself immediately with his equal will-spirit that has penetrated the whole soul. And then he is completely one with it, just as God is and remains one with it, although on an infinitely higher level.

Once man has accomplished this, his thought, with which he has transferred himself even to the most distant region, is no longer an empty thought without effect. Spiritually it transfers to that place the whole being of such a perfected man, who is now able to perform everything. He sees, hears and perceives everything, because with the endless will-spirit it penetrates and controls everything, without losing even for a moment its individual independence. Since it penetrates and controls everything, it can also, like a thought, filled with the true Spirit of God, perform everything in one moment whatever the perfect man wills.

But as long as man has not attained this most blessed and only true condition of divine life, he can only materialize his thoughts and ideas imperfectly in one way or another, through the members of his body, and this only according to the laws of nature, that is under judgment.

2.4 The perfect human being

There is only one God, one life, one light, one love and only one eternal truth, and our present life on Earth is the path to it. We have proceeded out of love and out of light, through the will of the eternal love, in order to become an independent love and an independent light. We can do it; we must do it! How?

Through love for God and through its never-resting able activity! For our love for God is the love of God itself in us and directs our soul to the constantly rising activity of the true, the eternal life which is in itself the fullest truth and the brightest light.

With God all things are possible, so it is also possible for the most hardened worldly man and sinner to change himself quickly and efficiently, if he sincerely, in full faith and trust in God, does what the divine wisdom is advising him. He must then perform a true miracle on himself by a strict reversing of his will. This miracle is achieved by a total self-control of all his former weaknesses, habits, lusts and bad tendencies, which arise in his soul from the unfermented and very impure nature of his body, polluting and disfiguring him.

How many different worldly passions do you have?

Take a serious decision to overcome them all and then you will be on the way to God. If you can do that, then you will quickly obtain the inner life perfection; but if you cannot do that, life will be very difficult for you.

The will to sin finds in man always a lot of support, and more precisely in the tendencies of his body. The will to do what is good finds no support in the body. This could be found only in your heart and in the faith in a true God, and most of all in the love for Him, and also in the hope that the promises God has given will be completely fulfilled.

Therefore, one can battle against all the bad passions of his body, and in this way one will become master over himself, although one still will oftentimes not lack all kinds of temptation. This is the first degree of the true inner life perfection.

Then, through the firm and living faith, the love for God and fellowman and by the unwavering hope, he will soon become lord over the whole nature. In this degree, man has already received such great strength and life freedom, because in his soul he is completely filled with God's will and can act according to it. He will nevermore commit any sin, for when you become pure everything is also pure to you.

Although man is then already a perfect lord over the whole nature and has within him the complete conviction that he can sin no more, because all his actions are guided by the true wisdom out of God, yet he still remains thereby in the second degree of the inner life perfection.

But there is still a third and most high degree of inner life perfection. Of what does it consist, and how can we attain it?

It consists in the fact that the perfect man, who knows very well now that he is a powerful lord of the whole nature, and which can do whatever he wants, still, in a humble and meek way, controls his willpower and might, and in all his actions, out of pure love for God, only waits until he receives from God an assignment. This is, for the perfect lord of nature, a very difficult task, because in his full wisdom, always realizes that according to the will out of God that lives in him, he can only do the right thing.

But an even more profound spirit will also realize that between the special will of God in him and the most free and endless universal will in God there is still a big difference, by which he makes his special will completely subordinate to the universal divine will, and will only do something of his own power when he directly receives an assignment for it from the will of God. He, who does that, has attained within him the innermost and highest life perfection, and this is the life perfection in the third degree.

Whoever has obtain it is also completely one with God and possesses, just like God, the highest might and power over everything in Heaven and on Earth, and nobody can ever take it away from him, because he is completely one with God.

Nobody can reach this highest life perfection wherein the archangels are, before achieving the first and second degree of life perfection.

To become equal to God means: to become full of love for your fellowmen, and to let your heart be full of humility, meekness, patience and mercy regarding everybody. Then God will also have mercy on you, and in the spirit of His love and eternal truth He will let Himself to be found by you.

If you only want to search God in and with only the truth, then you will find Him indeed, but you will not see His real being and even less understand it. However, if you are searching God in the pure love, humility, meekness, patience and mercy, then you will find God, recognize Him and receive the eternal life of your soul.

2.5 *Two categories of human souls*

There are two kinds of people on this Earth, most of them are entirely of this earth on account of the systematic gradual progress of the soul through the various kingdoms of nature, and they can be called "children of this Earth".

However, a much smaller number of people living here are of this planet only where their bodies are concerned, but their souls are either from various stellar worlds or, sometimes, they are even pure angel spirits from the spirit-heavens, and they can be called "children of Heaven".

It is these who are capable of grasping the secrets of the Kingdom of God and of passing them onto the children of the Earth through teaching, so they can also become children of Heaven and citizens of the Kingdom of Heaven.

Well, these worldly people, once they have grown out of the mud of this Earth, are naturally still very much of a sensual nature, since their souls have never gone through any sort of human preparatory schooling of a free, self-determining life. In the beginning, they can only be taught through sensual images about the realization of a very high and eternal spirit of God.

For the sake of most of the people of this Earth the revelations about the kingdom of the spirits are clothed in somewhat sensual images, which can be revealed by the children of Heaven only from time to time, more and more, according to the ability of the children of the Earth to understand – but never too much at one time, but instead only as much as they are capable of bearing and digesting in their spiritual "stomachs".

Then, the question for sure arises in your mind: "Am I also from above?"

Those from this world are only allowed to hear about God's miracles and certainly not see them; for if they would see such big signs it would kill them completely, spiritually speaking. Therefore, they must only grow on God's words.

However, there also will be a sign given to them, but no other than this of the prophet Jonah; since he only spend three days in the belly of the fish and then was put ashore alive, also

Christ spent three days in the grave and then emerged alive again, to the biggest fright and judgment for those down there.

The children of this Earth can only be won for the Kingdom of God through the living word and not by signs! Since the most children of this Earth – if not already spoiled through all kinds of false signs – are gullible but not obtuse and therefore can soon and easily be won for the truth through a right speech; but through too strikingly signs, they would entirely lose their ability to exercise their free will.

When she is embodied on this Earth, the soul from above retains in its flesh certain feeling from where she originates and turns the ears and especially the eyes towards that direction from where she originally descended from. People who like to turn their eyes up, to beautiful things, and listen to those harmonious sounds, which are coming from above to their ears, are most certainly from above. People, who direct their eyes mainly to the ground and rummage in it to look for all kinds of treasures and only seldom turn their ears and eyes upwards, are most certainly from below. According to this, if you pay attention to it, you can clearly recognize whom you have in front of you.

People who are from above are normally very inventive and they are producing all kinds of arts and sciences; but many of them are more or less difficult believers, since they want everything very clearly to be proven.

The weak small children of this Earth soon and easily believe everything what they are presented to believe, and only require the explanation afterwards, once they accumulated a large supply of believe principals. With them however one should pay close attention, that only the purest truth is preached to them; woe him, who wants to annoy the little ones of this earth with all kinds of false examples and teachings! But with the children from above the explanation must be either already given in advance or at least at the same time when the teaching is given, otherwise they will not easily accept anything else than the full truth.

The Word firstly illuminates the mind of a person, the mind then awakens the will and the love in a person's heart and love becomes a mighty flame. This illuminates and enlivens the will in the heart and acts according to the prescription of mind, and what a person does freely out of himself is a rewarding deed, and only then man can find his own life cooker.

The miraculous sign however strikes the human mind down for a long time and startles only love and its will to act. But this action is similar to a stone thrown through the air, which flies through the air for as long as the throw strength is bigger compared with the drawing force of the mass; however, as soon as this strength diminish, the stone falls on to the ground as dead and immovable and remains there in its old judgment.

The soul of a person converted by a sign resembles entirely the thrown stone. That person acts blindly out of fear for the sign and the love and will of the soul weakens, especially with the descendants who have seen no signs, and becomes totally sluggish and regards the sign either as a piece of magic or as a flat lie and invention of the ancestors.

Are we then less human than our ancestors, who received all kinds of signs and then could easily believe? We now should believe what we do not understand and the signs which we only hear about, should now serve us as a motive to believe? No, this is fundamentally wrong! A wise God, if there is one, never ever demand this from us! Therefore, we also demand signs or at least such an explanation, which gives us a right light about what we should believe and what we should do, so that we can recognize the right reason. We demand such believe motives, which for all people at all times appeared as effective, not the ones we were coerced to believe.

This is how the mind of man reasons, and this is rightly so! If the teaching with the given signs is not put in the right light for the human mind, soon it sinks with all signs and the people are losing in the process all faith and fall in their old, sluggish and wild life, until a clever magician comes to them and brings them soon and easily on his empty side.

2.6   The right spiritual guidance

There certainly are unheard of abominations taking place constantly, some of them being initiated by the so-called servants of God! And mankind, bound to hear about it, increasingly ask one another daily: "What's this? What is the word of God? Can it be God's will, and purpose of His teaching, that the proclaimer of God's Word, grace, gentleness and peace should be the most greedy, domineering, selfish, loveless and impudent devils towards their fellowmen?

These are good questions, for these are the first impulses towards peoples' true independence of action, without which they can never go over into true spiritual freedom, either through benevolence and even less so through evil and so-to-say hellish coercion, for without spiritual freedom there can be no eternal life for the soul and its spirit.

It is true, when observing the actions of some of our fellowman, including some of the priesthood, one can shear of just annoyance and nearly get completely dissolved by it and one often would like to scream at top of one's voice: "Lord! Don't You have no lightening, no hail, no sulfur and no pitch anymore, to punish these people-tigers with the most severe sharpness of Your divine rage?" But then a gentle voice from the innermost heart says: "Be clever and wise, and watch your step! If you see an adder lurking next to the road, sidestep it! For the whole earth is not yet covered by adders!

It has to be night just as there is day, so that people can recognize the value of light. During the day no person has any need for the light of a lamp; but if it gets night then every person feels painfully the absence of light and gets himself a light as best he can and even a weak luster makes his room more friendly then a total lack of light.

If the Lord provides the people of this earth with all kinds of goods, they soon become wanton and start to provide too much for their body. Their soul, in which the divine spirit resides, will soon be consumed, instead of obtaining in the right measure the strengthening from the body for the germination of the divine spirit to an everlasting life, as such is prescribed by God, and for which final purpose God actually has given the soul a body. However, if the soul has been consumed by its body, instead of noble fruits, only thorns, thistles and all kinds of evil weeds appear, from which surely no grapes and figs can be harvested!

Such a person is then spiritually as good as dead! He doesn't know anything about the spirit. He denies everything spiritual and materializes everything. Except for coarse matter, nothing else exists for such a person; his stomach and his sensuous skin are the only two divinities for which he is day and night prepared to bring any sacrifice.

For such a person, no God exists anymore. If such people finally become priests and servants of God (as it is unfortunately very often the case today) one should not ask himself: "Why these servants of the flesh (for whom the soul, spirit and God and His heavens are nothing more than outdated, poetically fantastic pictures of speech) have become priests and servants of

God?" Instead, one has to look only at their oversized bellies and one has the fullest answer vividly before one's eyes!

For these broadcasters of the word of God it is just the same whether they satisfy their entrusted congregational with bread from the heavens or with the mud from nauseating puddles; as long as they are paid majestically well! Therefore, we should not be too surprised, if from time to time we hear things from the church, which quite often makes us becoming nearly stiff from terror.

If a person has regressed to a level which is less then mushroom of the forest, growing out of mud, for the worthiness to be a human being, what nobleness can be expected from such a mud-person? One should let him live like a disgusting adder lurking and hissing next to the road and look for any adder-less place on the wide surface of mother earth. For the Lord is with everybody who truly is searching for Him, and does not abandon him, who in his misery turns to Him!

Spiritually, the people of this Earth are like the garden soil, and the Word of God (which initially came through our forefathers from the heavens, starting with Adam and later the patriarchs and prophets, awaken by God Himself) is like the precious and good seeds, which is laid into the soil of the little garden. But just as no seed laid into the earth at once becomes the new, many fold, ripe fruit, just so is it also with the Word of God.

When the word of God, through hearing, enters man's heart, it must, as commanded by God's word, be enlivened through good deeds towards our brothers and sisters, which are akin to the enlivening nutrient powers of the soil, and thereby brought to proper germination for the purpose of the true and full strength fruit of spiritual life in God, therewith becoming a fully blessed and fully ripened fruit! However, if people (foremost those who take up God's word, like prophets and priest) instead to let it ripen in themselves (and sow it in its fullest genuineness into the large field of all people of this earth for all times of times) consume it themselves, like the earth which fatten itself with the noble seed, and use it as a mean for their own fattening alone, then of course no wonder that on the large human field only weeds, thorns and thistles germinate and reach evil ripeness!

Notwithstanding the fact that it happens so, it is not against God's order and wisdom, when the choice fruit ripens, the straw and all fruit is gathered into the barns, the weeds being left in the field, spontaneously manuring the soil which is then fortified for subsequent sowing, to avidly take up a fresh seeding and enliven it.

So it is also with us humans. If we have from all times past been satisfied with the most pure truth as it comes forth from the mouth of God, we should have very little craving after more new truth!

God the Lord foresees this however and allows a dulled mankind to be served up pigs' fare for a while, and its soil to be much fortified through weeds; only then does mankind, languishing and pining after light in the night, enjoy the pure, and precious fruit of the pure Word of God, as is now the most obvious and blessed case among us.

In any case, this does not work with a similar speed for a more worldly- minded people as you imagine. Often, much time and patience is needed in order to purify a soul from all ashes. But before such a total purification can be successful, there is not too much to be done with the spiritual base, because to occupy the mind with this actually means to build a house on the sand.

The heart must seize the issue; but if it is still full of material things, the purely spiritual cannot find any starting point. Therefore, you must above all ensure that your heart is fully free of everything that is material.

Life is certainly a battle, but not an exclusively external one, but a quite powerful inner one against the outside! The external person must in the end be completely conquered by the internal one; otherwise, the inner person dies along with the external body! Let the inner person put a bridle on your fleshly tongue, so that it will rest and let the inner tongue of thoughts of the soul become active and recognize how misty and unclear things are in your house of life!

Do not concern yourself with all the external appearances; for little depends on whether one understands their reason or not! But recognize the true reason for the inner life of the soul and the spirit and everything will matter a lot to you and to every person!

3   ABOUT ANGELS

Every angel has the power to achieve at once everything that God can achieve unlimitedly Himself. But still, no angel does anything out of himself, but only when he receives the assignment from God. Therefore, even the highest angels are asking God to assign them to do this or that, especially when they can see that the people of this Earth are lacking one thing or the other.

Humans and Angels are distinguished from each other, in that Angels had used their freedom wisely since the primordial times, within God's order and had thereafter not ever sinned against it. Nevertheless, a proportion of spirits, too vast for our understanding, had misused their free will and therefore plunged into the threatened judgment. The natural men of this Earth as well as those of all other worlds is from such spirits, of which this whole Earth and all countless worlds, such as sun, moon and stars consist. And this along the familiar way of generation and subsequent birth, having to therefore first be reared and later instructed in human-hood and, after shedding of the body, developed into pure and completely free spirits.

Since the flesh of man is given him and therefore to the spirit raised up from judgment, mainly to undergo a free will test as if in a separate world, then for the angels, a body of flesh would be quite superficial, as the flesh is only the means but not and never can be the purpose, as everything is to ultimately become purely spiritual and never material again.

This Earth and this whole physical Heaven such as suns, moons and planets, shall once pass away, after all the spirits held captive within them shall through the way of the flesh have become pure spirits, and the pure spirits remain forever like that and shall not and cannot ever pass away.

None of the angels from the Heavens are capable, just as little as you men on Earth, to accomplish anything out of themselves. They are in a certain way the fingers on His hand and the executioners of His will. Therefore, they are free beings, as if not limited by anything, being an outflow themselves of the divine power and they can therefore accomplish all that this power reveals and wills in them, and what they then accomplish is not their work, but only that of the Lord.

They are completely independent and also completely free in every respect, but since the greatest completeness exists only and solely in the wisdom and the will of the Lord, it is obvious that not only a human being but especially an angel spirit – who is also only a being – will be more and more independent and free according to the measure that he made the wisdom and the will of the Lord as his own.

And the more they make the will of the Lord as their own, the more free might, power and authority will be theirs, and they can also accomplish everything and bring forth what the Lord Himself can accomplish and bring forth.

Nevertheless, an angel is also a receptacle and not just a purest beam of divine will. He feels very well what he wants, and then what the Lord wants. He perceives the Lord's will more easily, distinctly and quickly than humans, and he is instantly and completely surrenders his will to the will of the Lord. Therefore, he can just as well be regarded as a pure emanation of the divine will; but he has nevertheless a wholly free will and could, just like a man, act contrary to the Lord's will. Yet, this could hardly happen because each angel possess such a high degree of wisdom so as to be able, as a spontaneous light out of the divine primal light, to recognize only too well the eternal, immutable justice of the divine will as the greatest value of life of all men, angels and worlds.

3.1 The guardian angels

Everyone shall be living in accordance with his beliefs and loves, because at any moment man is free to call upon God for protection, and God shall turn His countenance towards him who pleads and help him in every adversity.

Besides that, everyone has been assigned a guardian angel who has to guide him from his birth to his grave. Such a guardian angel always influences a person's conscience and only begins to keep further and further away from his ward when the latter, guided by his self-love, has voluntarily relinquished all faith and all love for his neighbor.

Thus the men on this Earth are by far not as forsaken as you think, for everything depends on their free will and actions, whether they wish to be supervised and guided by God, or not. If they wish it, God will wish it too, but if they do not wish it, they are absolutely free as far as God is concerned and God does not take any further notice of them, except that they receive what according to universal order every natural being is destined to have as the natural life and what is needed to support it. But that is as far as God will and can go with such a person because of his inviolable freedom. Only when a man with his heart's free will seeks and implores Him, God will always come to meet such a man on the shortest possible way, provided he seeks and prays in downright earnest.

But if a person only seeks and prays tentatively, in order to convince himself whether where God and His promises are concerned there is anything to it, he will not be considered by God or his prayer granted. For God is in himself the purest love and looks only upon those who come to Him in their heart's pure love and seek Him for His own sake, wish to learn to know Him with gratitude as their Creator and have the fervent wish to be guarded and guided by Him, personally.

As concerns those who come to God in this way, He knows every moment only too well how things are with them, and He teaches and guides them personally in everything. However, God certainly does not take any notice about those who want nothing to do with Him. And when, once in the beyond, they will be standing before God, calling fervently and saying: "Lord, Lord", God will answer them: "Out of My sight, you strangers, for I have never known you!" And such souls will then have to suffer and struggle considerably until they will be able to approach God as recognized by Him.

The angels are those who have to care for everything that concerns the being of a person from its birth to its departure from this Earth. They are those who purify the souls through the suffering and pain worked in their flesh, making them capable of receiving the Spirit of God, and they know and help us passing our diverse sufferings and pains.

The angels are also capable of feeling pain and suffering. They often bear more pain and suffering than humans, since they often have to experience how the stubborn people crush all their great efforts with scorn and mockery, under their dirtiest feet and constantly turn their backs on them.

The guardian angel has a divine patience with his guarded person and constantly showered him or her with the greatest good deeds. Unfortunately, many times that person disrespects him extremely for all that and didn't want to hear or know anything about him. The person only constantly directed all his thoughts away from his guardian angel, and striving basically to getting rid of him, who is his greatest do-gooder and friend.

Sometimes, with this kind of behavior, it is possible even to harm the guardian angel, despite all his cares and efforts for his salvation.

What it will do a man to such a person? Will he have the patience to treat such a villain right until the end with all patience and measure and tenderness? The angels have always such patience with the people of this Earth, through their own free will, even that they could decide to leave them alone in an instant, without any consequences for their angelic life.

Plus, consider the continuing willful behavior of the ones which are evil on purpose, who are sometimes spiritually speaking very powerful beings, and who are constantly going around with the "laudable plan to destroy not only the angels, but God as well, and to take away all His power!" Such a thing can never happen, of course! But the evil plan is there and they do not stop trying to carry it out, constantly suffering the greatest pain and agony for it, which they cause themselves through their most evil desire; but that never totally puts off their evil activity.

The angels have the power not only to tame them all, in the most sensitive way, but also to destroy them completely, forever, and all that without any responsibility before God! Nonetheless, the angels choose to treat them as their fallen brothers, with all patience and consideration and direct things strictly so that their free will is never limited by anybody in any way, but is and remains always free.

The angels could just as well leave everybody behind, according to their own freest will; but they are constantly chosen to stay with us, because such a thing pleases the Lord, and pleasing the Lord is their own free will.

3.2   *About life and sexuality of angels*

In the primordial spirits the male-positive being is without exception prevailing; nevertheless, in each one of them also the female-negative principle is fully present, and as such every angel in himself represents the most perfect marriage of the heavens of God. It entirely depends on each one of them, if they want to show themselves in either the male or female form.

Moreover, therein lays also the reason that they never can get old, because both poles continuously support each other forever. In humans the poles are separated in a sexually personality, and because each pole exists on its own, they do not have any support in themselves.

With angels everything they take in is totally consumed and transformed into visible life – with man only what corresponds to the isolated life-polarity, whilst the incompatible part is removed through the natural process.

The angels have the word of God from eternity in them, just like heavens and all creation consists of this very Word and are everywhere filled with it; and this Word is primarily their being-like being and for such being also the only, most true life-bread and the true life-wine.

In every angel it is the spirit of the Lord who acts, works and does everything, who actually makes and fills their innermost being; for angels are basically nothing other than focus of the rays of the divine spirit! They are in a certain way the personified, powerfully active will of God; their word is the speech of His mouth and their beauty is a little reflection of His endless magnificence and always immeasurable majesty.

If Jesus is also infinite in his majesty of wisdom and power, he is nonetheless a limited person in the love of the Father. And exactly this love, which makes Him a person before us, also makes the angels to live for us, otherwise they are only light and fire, darting through all the infinite space as great, creative thoughts, filled with the word, the power and the will from eternity!

And if you are already so much taken aback with this, what would you say about the truth that, on the entire Earth, only one angel is assigned the task of caring and acting upon all the grass, shrubbery and trees for the bringing forth of all the most diverse fruits, as well as take care of all the animals of the sea, air and upon the land?

3.3   *Angels and Humans*

Angels always follow most precisely the will of the Lord; only what He wants is good and this is what they do! If it would be beneficial for the nascent people of this earth and necessary for their soul salvation, they always would be visible among the people; but this is not the case, and therefore they are only allowed to guide the people unseen, so that their free will does not suffer any force. This is the Lord's love, wisdom and will, and therefore everything must take place, exist and be accordingly; if something does not take place, exist and be, it is as good as a pure nothingness. However, if the people from now on will live and act as the Lord wants, after laying off their material body they will also become what angels are now; since also they were once on a celestial body, the same as we are now.

On the other hand, even the least person of this earth is already in the cradle many times more than angels are in all greatness, wisdom and power, since the right people of this earth are the children of the pure everlasting love of God, and the highest wisdom and power must develop in them totally free out of their love for God, their truest Father. The angels have gone forth as creatures of His wisdom, therefore they must first out of their great wisdom create the love for God in themselves, which is nearly incomprehensible more difficult than for love of God find the highest wisdom and power in oneself.

For that reason the people of this earth have emerged from the pure love in God, thus themselves are the love in God. The angels, as Wisdom creatures, are not allowed to bother us in our free development out of our primordial love of God in our being. This is the reason why the angels of God are not allowed to surround us in their visible form. They are only allowed to awake the sleeping wisdom and power in our love for God, very gently and unnoticed, but never ever breathe only one single spark from their actual wisdom into us; since this would not awake our wisdom, but only suppress it.

This is also the case among the earth people. Since what would become of a child, if you take it from the nurse and immediately put into high school, where highly wise and highly learned teachers present to their properly prepared scholars the deepest and (for the ordinary person) fully incomprehensible sciences and secret arts? In the end, such a child would be able to repeat its teacher's words, but never understand the deep sense and its meaning. Therefore, let the children first be educated by the nurse and guide it through all kinds of play to the first, child-like thinking. From year to year the child then becomes riper and more prepared for a higher education.

What we do with our children, the angels do with us, and must do it therefore, because the people of this earth are children of the Lord.

If a man had been born on the world on which the angels once lived in the flesh, that man would already have all the necessary wisdom and would nearly need no other education, but only to find the love to God in the light of his great wisdom.

Look at all the animals of the Earth! They are also creatures of the wisdom of God; therefore, they also do not require any education, whereby they troublesome have to learn what they have to do according to their abilities and nature, but they bring all this with them during birth and are immediately in their particular way a perfect artist. Whoever taught the bees herbalism, who showed them where the honey is located inside the flowers, and where the wax? Who taught them to build their cells and to produce inside their bellies fragrant honey from sweetish flower nectar? Where did the spider learn to prepare its thread and to weave a highly useful net? See, all this is provided to the animals by the wisdom of God, whose products are only for the time being. But because they are only that, they have that what they have in the highest perfection, but since they nearly totally lack love and its free will, they cannot learn much additionally.

There nevertheless exist animals, to which already certain symptoms of higher love have been so to speak mixed in. And see, such animals are therefore already able to accept some side training from the people and thus can be trained for certain tasks. And the more love is present in certain animals, like for example dogs or some birds, the more the ability of such animals for a better training for different tasks.

Now, this however is in the highest degree the case with human creatures from other world bodies, because they are coming to earth with all thinkable abilities already provided. They don't need to learn too much in school. But since love only develops in time as a product of their wisdom, on this other world bodies they nevertheless have schools, where it is taught how one, out of pure wisdom, can attain free love and a free will. If such a person has managed to reach such goal with a lot of hard work, only then he is able to get close to God and also to His children of this earth.

And hence you again can see a little clearer why the people of this earth are not allowed to have a continuous visible contact with angels during the development of their wisdom. In short, our task is to develop and search for wisdom out of love, and the angels" task is to search and develop the love for God out of wisdom.

Who manages to become a perfect child of God – which really requires a lot – is of course endlessly happy; but the angels are also perfectly content with their lot, and do not require anything more or higher!

Men have been called and designated to become in fullest independence; for us the Lord said: „You must become perfect in everything, even as your Father in heaven is infinitely perfect!

Now you are certainly embryos in the womb which cannot build any houses with the smallest strength of life that you have been given; but when you are reborn out of the true womb of the spirit, then you will also be able to act as the Lord acts! The Lord will say to you: "I did great things before you, but you will do even greater things before the whole world!

The God's endless love, mercy and extremely great compassion determine a way for the angelic spirits, on which they will become fully equal to the children of God. The path which the Lord Himself now treads will become the path of all original spirits of all the heavens – but certainly not from one day to the next, but instead gradually, in an evenly continuing unfolding of the never-ending eternity, in which the angels from God move up and down as if in an endlessly great circle, without ever touching the outer edge of the circle. But even if something must be waited for a long time, it nonetheless happens in the end because it is kept faithfully and true in the great order of the Lord. Once it has happened, it is there, as if it had been there since eternity.

4   ABOUT DEVILS

Can there be a human soul which in the end loses itself so much that it begins to deny its own being quite seriously and can no longer be convinced that it exists?

Yes, when that situation occurs with the people of the world then man has completely stopped being human; he is then only an instinctively reasoning animal and above all incapable of any further education of the soul and the spirit. Thus such a body must be killed and decay along with a large part of the too intensively incarnated soul, so that maybe after many millennia a soul which has become free of that incarnation can enter the path to its self-education and independence, either on this Earth or on another.

However, people who no longer know anything about their own soul for pure concern about the world and their flesh, you can recognize partly in yourself, partly in the great part of all people; for no-one knows any longer who and what the soul is! One talks about it and says: "With heart and soul!" and "He is my soul mate!"; but if you ask someone: "Friend, who and what is the soul?" - the person questioned stands there like an ox on a mountainside not knowing what to say!

Once a soul does not recognize herself any longer and in the end even quite forgets what and how she is, then everything ends! And there is nothing left for God to do, except the old maneuver of destroying the human being, sometimes to a large degree, sometimes to a lesser degree, depending on the situation of the people whether they still know something about their soul and spirit, or nothing at all.

Such worldly and fleshly people may look very beautiful and sumptuous, particularly the female sex; the easily understandable reason lays in the constant greater conjunction of the soul with the body. But such people also become weak through this and are very susceptive to all serious physical effects. Their bodies become sick easily and the slightest wind of a plague brings inevitable death, while people who have a free soul and a free spirit can let all the poisons of the Earth come over them and it will not harm them in the least; for a free soul and the freest spirit in her have power and means in abundance to face every enemy in the most effective way, while a soul gagged everywhere by her cursed flesh resembles a tied-up giant who in the end cannot even defend himself against a fly and has to allow an insensible dwarf with a knife to slowly but painfully remove his head from his body.

Every man who turns to evil and away from the divine order does so at first spontaneously. In most cases, the fault lays in a wrong upbringing. This encourages him to indulge in evil passions which, in turn, lead to all sorts of real transgressions. Through these he also throws himself wide open to all unknown evil influences and can thus be – and remain – depraved down to the foundation of his inner life, but always only if he wants to!

If he is willing to reform, the Lord does not prevent him from doing so; for as soon as someone in distress feels the slightest inner desire for help, he is soon given it. However, if he is quite comfortable and contented in his evil ways and never, be it silently or openly, expresses a desire for betterment, he is not given the extra help for his will.

To be sure, the good is whispered to the sensory organ of his heart, called "conscience", and from time to time he is quite severely reprimanded from above. If he heeds the admonitions at least to some degree, he can no longer become lost or depraved. In this case, the secret help keeps coming from above, giving the soul insight and strength so that she can extricate herself more and more from the entanglement. And it is then only a matter of good will and progress will be made – at least to a point where the man, ready for a higher revelation, is seized by the Spirit of God Himself and from then on guided in the true light of life.

Yet if man, in his gross delusion and worldly-sensual enjoyment, does not in the least heed the gentle and soft admonitions coming from above and manifesting in the heart, but acts as if he were lord over the whole world – well, surely, nobody else can be blamed for the incorrigible state of his soul but this very soul herself.

There are no so-called original devils in the whole natural and spiritual world, but instead only those who previously have lived on the world as incurably bad and evil people; they not only enticed other people to all sorts of burdens and disgracefulness, but also used with them all the means of force at their disposal – whereby they spread an even greater damnation in themselves, which they will find it difficult to ever fully get out of.

You can well imagine that in the beyond the Lord, in accordance with the established order, will allow all sorts of things through which a depraved soul can be healed. For the Lord has not created any soul for perdition, but for the highest possible perfection of life. Yet bear in mind also that not a single soul in the whole endless space of creation can attain perfection of life through some sudden, implicit act of mercy, but only through its efforts based on its very own volition. The Lord puts many an aid at man's disposal; but man has to recognize them as such, seize them with his own will and use them quite voluntarily.

Yes, when a man then spontaneously exclaims in his heart: "Lord, I am too weak to avail myself of the means which You gave me; help me by lending me Your arm!" – ah, then man has himself asked for the help from above of his own will, recognizing and perceiving the inadequacy of his own strength. Then the Lord can act immediately with all the necessary might and power and promptly help that weak soul.

In this case, man's will as well as his cognition and trust must be accompanied throughout by the fullest determination. Otherwise, that order would prevail, according to which each soul had to help herself by use of the available means; for every outside interference with the intrinsic element of the free will would obviously and necessarily lead to a dissolution of the soul's essence.

Neither God nor an angel will come to Earth saying to everyone: "Look, eat this and that if you are hungry!". Instead, the hunger comes and the person tastes with his palate the fruit growing everywhere and those that taste good to him he will seize and quiet his hunger with them very comfortably. If he is thirsty, he hurries to a fresh spring and if he is cold he will soon sew together a cover out of all sorts of fine material that does not itch and scratch his skin and thus protect his skin from the coldness of the air. And if he wants to be protected from the rain and wild animals, he will soon complete a hut; for all sorts of means have been given to him for this. Wherever he turns, he finds immediately some knack which he easily recognizes as such and can then use just as easily with the powers given to him for this.

The same principle applies, according to the eternal, necessary order of the Lord, to the soul which has to develop independently. The soul must develop and perfect herself with the means available, just as every man on earth must himself search for his body's nourishment and must recognize and enjoy it in order to sustain his physical life.

4.1   About Lucifer

Christ, as Jesus, stood there alone and called Lucifer before Him, the fallen archangel, for whose sake all this was created. And Lucifer stood there in the form of a beautiful young man before Him, but without brilliance, with his head bended, waiting for His word. Christ said to him: "Bearer of light, You were not able to see the deity, but could only feel Him. When you went out from the middle of My love to create love and light in all the spaces of eternity, you believed that you were not the carrier but the possessor of that power. You changed your love into pride and said: "A God that cannot be seen is no God. The created beings that exist by my will honor me as the only visible being, as God. Therefore I want to be and stay God for them."

Then My voice called within you, and said: "The fullness of My Spirit works with you and in you, and all the qualities that are in Me form a ladder, upward and downward into infinity. I want to give you a part of My power, so that each one will rule from his most inner limits which form a point that lays deep inside, flowing out of infinity from two sides. So, while you came forth as a finite being from Me, you still can be infinitely active with Me, as antipode that stands justified before Me."

But you did not heed the warning and your power created numberless beings out of yourself, and they followed you and became mighty because I did not want to destroy the newly created beings that were a part of you. That multitude became bigger and bigger and they made you their god. Then you sinned again and said: "I am God, for nowhere do I see the power that creates something". Fool, as if the finite could ever see and understand the infinite!

Then I shackled you, and see that same Power stands here personally before you and says to you: "I am the God that was not visible up to now. Do you recognize Me now? Return to your Father's house, so that you will be freed from your shackles and occupy the place that belongs to you. See here those of them that kneel down before Me, who are set free from you, made innerly alive by My breath and who are dedicated to Me forever. Give up your pride! Let the warmth of My love blow in you, and then all matter will disintegrate into nothing!"

Lucifer said: "You are Jesus from Nazareth, a man with great power, which also I once possessed. But to recognize God, the highest power, the infinite in the finite, in You, no, never! What happened to me can also happen to others. Human beings are mortal, their bodies will rot. This is what will also happen to you, your body will dissolve, and only dust will be left over from Jesus.

I know my guilt and I see that I am stripped of my brilliance, and I give you also these few that are mine, who are following you there. But the almightiness will never consider destroying His creation, which is actually my work, which I actually gave to Him and which I love also, just like Him, for it is out of me. Let the battle continue, for only by this battle life exists. The horror of death is my work, and by that I keep my creatures with me, and they stay with me so that my qualities can live in them. So, it is good as it is. Then, what do you still want from me?"

Christ, as Jesus, then said: "This is not the place to argue, for you very well know what it is all about. I, as Son of Man, received all power from the Heavens, and only your hardness does not want to recognize Me, because you still hope to overcome the Deity, to overpower Him. You interpret His great tolerance as a weakness, His love as powerlessness. You do not want to let your multitude loose, for whose salvation I have covered Myself now in the garment of matter, and you try to stir them up, although you know that your followers have become much weaker and smaller. You succeeded to capture the minds and turned them away from the knowledge. The existence of paganism is your work. However, despite all that, all your deeds turned out in such a way that the fallen ones were still led to Me – and all that is not sufficient to you?"

Lucifer said: "Those who fell to you only await my call to come back. Give me the opportunity to prove to You how weak they are. And when I loose, I will acknowledge you. Give me power over your body, let me see the inner man that lives in you, then we will see how little divinity clings to it. And once Jesus will have paid His tribute to death, also these here will come back again to me, to whom they belong!"

Christ said: "What I will lead Myself into My Kingdom is lost for you forever. Since the beginning of time I know best which ways will lead to salvation. But beware, your measure is full! Out of love for the creatures of My Heavens and globes I came back, and out of love for them I will accomplish the work, despite your stubbornness.

Do not boast about the fact that with your destruction also the destruction of all the created beings out of you are sealed, so that their time also depends on yours. The time will come when you will stand before Me, not only stripped of your brilliance like now, but also stripped of every being out of you, and then no created being will be affected by your destruction anymore. Then you will have to decide again, in case you do not prefer to come to Me earlier in your free will. But now go away from here, for My decision stands firm, and My will shall be done."

Then Lucifer disappeared, and Jesus Christ blessed those souls who stood around Him.

Now here is the moment to understand the following and explain very clearly who and what Lucifer actually is, how one should understand him and how he can be overcome in every individual, for only when these most important questions are correctly and clearly answered it is possible to understand the creation, Christ descend to this Earth, and His suffering and dying.

When the Deity had found Himself, through processes that will always remain hidden to us, being aware of His creative and all-encompassing Spirit, a mighty surging and pushing arose in Him and He spoke in Himself: "I want to put My ideas outside of Me, so that I will be able to see from this what My powers can do!" - for as long as there is no activity, the Deity can only know Himself in a small measure. It is only through His works that He becomes ever more aware of His power and rejoices in it (just like every master artist can only see from his own products what is in him and rejoices in it).

So, the Deity wanted to create, and spoke then to Himself: "In Me there is all power of the eternities. Let us therefore create a being who is equipped with all power, equal to Me, but in such a way that he will have the qualities in him in which I can recognize Myself." And a Spirit was created, who was equipped with all the power from God, to make visible to the Deity the powers that are in Him.

In this Spirit, the Deity Himself wanted to determine the fixed point of His own active power – just like a human being, when he walks, will only find a fixed point of support on the firm ground of the Earth, to activate his power to move forward. The resistance of the Earth itself is good, it is even the mean by which the power actually operates and by which a moving forward can take place. This power that was delivered, which was placed in the new Spirit that came into existence, was the antipode – wanted by the Deity – which means the contrast of all those qualities that you call divine. That antipode is therefore not outside the Divine, but makes it only possible to spread the right light of knowledge.

Because it must be possible for every quality, when perfect, to be viewed from two sides. God's perfection can be found where both sides fall into one point. Descending and ascending from this center point, they both lose themselves into infinity.

Take love for example, the highest law and the noblest quality in the center of God's heart. Everyone will easily perceive that a very loving person can increase further in his love; for it is clear that already on our Earth a more loving person can always be found. And nevertheless you will see that very loving people will also have the right antipode in them by which they are also capable to refuse, out of love and for wise reasons, all kinds of wishes if by that they were to harm those who came asking.

If one being was created and placed on that border from which he freely can develop oneself into both directions, it is easy to realize that one more and more will be able to develop the possibility in oneself to refuse. By that one will separate oneself more and more from the middle border and will finally loose oneself into the most endless depths of the antipode, meaning in extreme hardening. Thus, when you look at a bad person you always can imagine a person that is worse, with less love, who will lose himself in egoism, because of the extreme separation.

Now, if God created a being who possessed both poles of the divine qualities, it does not mean that God completely did away from them, so that God would in a way only exist out of one half. It only means that God created a being placed on that mentioned border, equipped with God almightiness with which he thus was active and whom God gave the freedom to develop himself upwards or downwards. And from that complete power, God let this Spirit to work freely.

That first light of knowledge – meaning the knowledge of the possibility to develop oneself upwards or downwards – should keep the being in the center out of his free will, be active from there in very close connection with the Divine Spirit and always create new beings with his own creative power, so that the Creator as well as the creature could truly delight in it and savor that joyful activity in a higher degree of blissfulness.

The name of this first created spirit is "Lucifer" (meaning "Bearer of light"). He carried within himself the light of knowledge, and as first spiritual being he was well aware of the limits of the inner spiritual polarities. Equipped with God complete power, he was able to call other beings to life, which were equal to him in everything. They also felt the Deity and saw the same light of knowledge lighting up in them, and they also were active with their own creative power and were equipped with all the power of God's Spirit. However, the seven special powers of God's initial Spirit were expressed in them, this means that for what concerns their character they became similar to God's seven most important qualities. But their being possessed one special characteristic among the seven, which made them the carrier of that special quality, for already in the very beginning God took care that His created beings would depend on each other by necessity – the best way to prevent them from becoming proud regarding each other.

Lucifer, who surely knew that, he developed the antipode of God in himself, and he felt into the misconception that he, as a finite being, could absorb the infinite into him. But here the law was also valid: "No one can see God (the infinite) and keep his life at the same time!" As a result of that, he could feel the essence of the deity and hear His commands as long as he was standing in the right center point, but he never could see Him personally.

Because a finite being can and will never understand the infinity, then the creature, regarding this point, easily fall into errors and by going down harden himself in these; so Lucifer fall, despite all warnings, into the delusion that he could capture and absorb the Deity. Through that, he left his right position, distanced himself from the center point of God's heart and fall ever more victim to the wrong wish to gather around him his beings – who existed by him, but out of God – in order to rule over the spaces that were inhabited by all kinds of beings.

Now, since there was a discord which means a separation of groups, this finally led in the withdrawal of the power that was given by God to Lucifer and his followers, and he became powerless and his creative power was taken away.

Of course, the question came up: "What will happen now with that multitude of fallen ones who were as if dead, that means without activity?" There were only two ways!

The first way: to destroy Lucifer with his followers and then create a second one, who would probably be subjected to the same error, since a more perfect spirit, completely set free out of God and therefore not dependent of His will, could not be created. To create machines without free will, that execute what God command was not difficult. But to acquire the light of self-awareness is the only way. Plus, the spirits which were created via Lucifer (but from God), and who remained loyal to him, they belonged to his sphere. A sudden destruction of Lucifer would thus also have resulted in the destruction of all living beings.

Imagine a person who puts his children and grandchildren around him, but who actually still owe their life to God. If the deeds, thoughts, and so on, of this person were destroyed forever, then also his descendants would be destroyed, since otherwise the remembrance to him would still live on in them. Only a complete erasing of everything that ever came into contact with him – independent whether this was good or bad and deserved to be destroyed or not – would make a complete purification possible.

But why should Lucifer deserve this, since his fall took only place because of a misconception by which the possibility existed to go away with that misconception? Why would have done those beings, that remained loyal to him, to deserved their destruction? And finally: where would be God's wisdom if would not have known and foreseen about the possibility of the fall? And most of all: where would be God's love if it would not hold back a destruction but rather find ways by its wisdom to bring the lost beings back to the light of knowledge, so that as a result they would remain in the right balance of the polar qualities? Therefore, it was useless to destroy everything in order to repeat the cycle of creation!

In conclusion, only the second way remain valid, which could be seen before us in the material creation.

Imagine a person who absolutely does not want to realize that the king of the country is a mighty ruler, since that person, although equipped with all power and authority received from that king, never saw him personally. He rebels against him and would raise himself to be king. In order not to bring to ruin the subordinates who remained loyal to him, the king grabs him, removes his splendor, takes away his authority and throws him in a locked chamber, just as long as it takes to let him come to reason, and he will do the same with the followers. They will be freed according to how much they will do penance, realize their error and firmly adhere to the king will, which is now also visibly to them.

This weak earthly image shows us what God had done, because the material creation is that imprisonment. Moreover, to understand the following, we must awake the intuition of our soul, because the human reason falls too short to understand this.

A soul is composed of numberless particles of which each one of them comes from an idea that originated from God, and once he has found himself he cannot become anything else anymore than what he is, because he then corresponds to the character that he accepted. When a crystal is crystallized, its characteristic cannot be changed anymore, and it crystallizes either as rhomboid, hexagon, octagon, and so on, according to the form of its nature, that means depending on how the parts are accumulated around its life's center.

Now, when there has to be a change, because the crystals did not end up completely pure, they have to be dissolved by warmth (love), to crystallize them out again during the cooling off of the warm love water which is the same as giving up their will. In this manner, every careful chemist will know how to obtain the most beautiful, clearest and biggest crystals that correspond to his purpose.

God is such a chemist. He dissolved the crystals that became impure (Lucifer and his followers) in the warm water of love and He let those souls crystallize out again to make them pure. This happened by the ascension through the mineral kingdom and the plant kingdom up to man kingdom. But, as the soul of Lucifer encloses the whole material creation, also that has to express itself in the form of a human being. That is why always all unions of spirits unite in one person, led by the leader of that union, and they form what is called the subtle sphere of that person. There is nothing similar on the material level, which expresses clearly this reality.

Now, Lucifer thinks that he must act the way it happens, so that matter could be created – a misconception because it is not matter that is the end goal of the Creation. But the only goal for the beings that were placed outside of God is to know the truth in freedom, to understand and to love the Deity. Matter is only the mean for that. Lucifer wanted to hold on to this second misconception and lost himself in the outer limits of his polar qualities, while he lied to himself that he had to maintain matter because of that. Enough freedom was given to him to penetrate matter, which means to consciously contemplate in himself so that the very first created Spirit would realize what kind of suffering he caused to his companions and by that he may turn around. But this he did not do and only from then on he wanted to rule as a king of matter that belonged to him. That is why he darkened as much as possible the human crystals, to maintain his kingdom, because the battle with God seemed great, exalting and life sustaining to him.

The human crystals, that also had to be set free again in order to attain the ultimate goal, could be inclined to him or to God, and during their life they repeatedly fell into his nets. Look at paganism in which he let himself be honored as king, and honor his polar qualities, which also contain great wisdom, as gods.

During the imprisonment, the reproach was always made: "If I just could see the king, I would believe in him" - and this became the reason for Christ incarnation, firstly for those who fell, and secondly to make the deity personally visible to those who did not fall, and so to award their faith.

Herein lays the secret of Christ incarnation, which had to break through matter that otherwise, had to become harder and harder in case Lucifer would lose himself ever more in the hardness of his antipode. Therefore, Christ incarnation showed very precisely the way to be free from idol worship and the worship of the polar qualities. And also, firstly proof had to be given that death (by which people became attached to matter and its pleasures) can be overcome and this is the highest goal that can be reached, and secondly that life does not take place in matter but in spirit, and that the matter is only a prison for the spirit.

4.2 About Satan

The endless space contains matter, which is under divine judgement and therefore fixed by the power of God's will. If this would not be the case, there would be no sun, no moon, no Earth and certainly no created being in the great endless space. Then, there would be only God, contemplating His great thoughts and ideas.

However, since eternity God had placed His thoughts as it were outside of Himself, and by His almighty will He has provided them with a visible form. These embodied thoughts and ideas of God are however strictly speaking not bodies, but they are spiritual things that are judged, and vessels for the ripening of an independent being. Thus, they are created beings, intended to exist continuously forever out of them and out of their own power, next to God, the Creator who could become visible to them.

All creatures which are judged beings, compared to the already pure and free spiritual ones, are still impure, unripe and therefore not yet good. Therefore, compared to the spiritual, pure and good, they can be regarded as bad and evil, as such.

Thus, by "Satan" one should understand the whole material creation in general, and by "devil" the separated specific parts thereof.

When a person in this world knows God's will and lives according to it, he raises himself out of the imprisonment that is inherent to all that which is material. In this way that person passes over to God's freedom that is inherent to everything which is spiritual.

However, a person who does not want to believe in God and consequently does not want to act according to His will that is revealed to man, sinks more and more and deeper into the created material and becomes spiritual impure, evil and maliciously judgmental, and consequently a devil. Because all that which is merely material and judged is – as already said – in relation to the free spiritual, which is pure and good. However, God didn't create something impure, bad and wicked, but something that is created for the sake of existence, gifted with intelligence and power of action and at the same time with a free will, in order to acquire independence in himself.

For God, there does not exist anything that is impure, bad or evil, because for the pure everything is pure. Everything that God has created is good, and therefore for God there is no Satan, no devil and consequently also no Hell. Only that which has been created as such is all that, as long as they have to remain something material and judged and as long as they finally, in possession of the free will, want to stay either good or bad.

So, when it is stated in the Scripture that Satan in the form of a snake has seduced the first human couple, it actually means to say that the first human couple who knew God's will very well, have allowed themselves to be enchanted by the material world and that the lust and the voice of their judged flesh said: "We want to see what will happen when we will act contrary to the well-known will of God. For God Himself has given us freedom to act. Therefore we cannot lose anything of our insight, but only win. Because God surely knows what can happen when we act freely. We however do not know it. Therefore, let us act only once according to our will, then we will know by experience that which God knows alone."

And then, both of them ate from the forbidden tree of knowledge by way of wanting to experience it themselves, and by that they sunk one degree deeper into their judged matter, which regarding to the free life of the spirit is also called "death".

After that, they realized very well that in their flesh dwells the bondage of judgment and death, because of a growing love for the world, who can bury the free soul in judgment and bondage. And so, they lost the pure paradise that consisted of the full union of the soul with his spirit. Then they could not find it back on their own, because their soul was wounded by the sting of matter and it took a lot of effort to maintain the soul above the judgment of the material bondage, as this is now the case with all the people. Therefore Christ came into this world as Jesus, namely to show the people again the true way of life and to give them back the lost paradise through his teaching.

This was also the same with Job. In an earthly way Job was an extremely happy man and possessed many things. He was however also a wise man and very dedicated to God, living strictly according to the law. However, his extreme wealth made his flesh more lusting and made high demands to the Spirit in him.

The judged flesh said in a way to the Spirit of Joy: "I want to see if my earthly pleasures and sorrow could draw you away from your God and if I could exhaust your patience in such a way that I could put you under my coercive judgment."

This gave Job a mighty battle to fight, because on the one hand all earthly pleasures were at his disposal, of which he indeed enjoyed, but they did not rule over his soul and he remained united with the spirit. Since in this way the evil spirit of matter could not achieve anything with the soul, his soul was tempted by all kinds of physical miseries that are symbolically described in the book. But Job endured them all with patience, although he now and then grumbled and was lamenting his misery. But he finally always recognized that before God has given him everything, and also God has taken it away and therefore He is the only one able to give it back to him, because of the full strengthening of his soul in the spirit.

Now, when this is so, then who was Satan who tempted the pious Job so much? It was the judged spirit of his flesh. This means the different lusts thereof.

But a certain personal primordial Satan and primordial devils did in reality not exist anywhere else, except in the judged worldly matter of all kinds. However, the reason why Satan and the devils were presented by the old wise men by all kinds of dreadful visions is that the soul had to be able to imagine through all kinds of terrible images what kind of misery a free life must suffer when she will allow herself to be recaptured by the judgment of matter.

4.3 About different kind of hells

Jesus caused the image of Satan to appear to his first disciples and they were extremely frightened. Something similar happened also a few times with the first fathers of this Earth. But during that time no explanation in words was given, because the elders, who were wise from the Spirit, understood very well the symbolic image by way of the inner correspondences and therefore they said: "It is terrible to fall into the hands of the judging God!" That means to say: it is terrible for a soul, who has already come to complete self-consciousness, to let himself be captured again by the unchangeable law of the coercing judgment of the godly will in matter.

The fact that this is described as something terrible for the soul can be learned by everyone from the experience of a dying person who did not attain to the complete rebirth of the soul. Because why is such a soul so much afraid of the death of his body? Because she – still being entangled in the coercing judgment of the body – thinks that she has to die together with the body.

That being the case, one can easily see this fear with all those who hardly believe, or not at all, in a continuance of life of the soul after the death of the body, because their souls is completely or for the greatest part in the judgment of their flesh, and consequently they have to experience death, as long as they are not completely separated from it by God's will.

Since you hopefully well understand now how things are with Satan and his devils, it will also become clear to you that things cannot be different with Hell. It is just like Satan, who is in himself the eternal coercive judgment, thus the world and the matter thereof.

And why is Satan also called a prince of darkness and the lie? Because matter is not what it seems to be! And he who in his love will grab it and allows himself to be captured by it, is then also clearly residing in the kingdom of the lie and, regarding the truth and the light of the spirit, in the kingdom of darkness.

He who for instance loves too much the so-called treasures of the kingdom of the dead matter and keeps them for what they seem to be and not for what they truthfully are, is by that already residing in the kingdom of the lie, because his love – the foundation of his life – is as it is completely blinded and sunken down in matter and will have great difficulty to raise himself up again, out of such a night towards the light of the full truth.

However, he who only considers gold as a corresponding form of expression which represents the good of the love in God, like pure silver represents the truth of the wisdom in God, knows therefore also the real value of gold and silver and is thus residing in the Kingdom of the truth, and his soul is not entangled in the treacherous appearance of the judgment thereof.

So also, with the elders and all prophets, gold, silver and the different kinds of precious stones had only the true meaning. But as matter however, they did not have any value, and for this reason they also could not become a danger for a soul. Through the discernment of the true value of the matter they discovered easily and quickly for what it could be suitable and useful and they derived the true benefit from it.

However, when in course of time the people bestowed the value to the matter because of their glitter and nice appearance, they passed over to its judgment, became spiritually blind, hard, greedy, stingy, untruthful, quarrelsome, deceitful, proud, malicious and lusting for war and conquest, and therefore they fell into idolatry and paganism, and consequently also in the actual Hell, out of which they could not be delivered without Christ.

For this reason, Christ had to cover Himself in matter and by that in the judgment, and He had to break through it, and by that He became the entrance gate to eternal life for all the people who had fallen, if they want to enter life through this gate.

Therefore, Christ is also the door to life and Life itself. Whoever will not enter inside through Christ, will not attain to life in the light of eternal truth and freedom, but will remain captured in the judgment of matter.

Now there is another question that comes up by itself, which sounds like this: are there really no personal Satan and personal devils?

Oh yes, they exist indeed, still living in the flesh, and even more so in the big world in the beyond, where always intent to exert a bad influence in the world on this side, because of the raw nature spirits with their predestined ripening still remaining in all kinds of matter. They notice very well the different weaknesses of humans and their inclinations, control and stimulate them to burning passions.

And once a weakness of a person has become a burning passion, he is already completely in the condition of the judgment of matter and its evil spirits, and then it is difficult for him to loosen himself from it.

Satan is the total sum of the total judged matter, and concerning his personality, strictly speaking it exists nowhere, but they have to be considered as an assembly of devils of all kinds, not only of this Earth but of all worlds in the endless space of creation, which are finally representing an immense great Cosmic Man.

Of course, on a smaller scale, an assembly of devils of a celestial body is also a Satan, and on the smallest scale every separate devil is it also in itself satanic.

However, as long as there were no men on a celestial body, there also were no personal devils, but only judged and unfermented spirits in all the matter of a celestial body. Matter is everything that can be observed with your sense organs.

But you also can trust that now no devils on any other celestial body are more evil and more malicious than precisely in and on this Earth. If it would be allowed to them, they would terribly harm the Earth and its inhabitants, but they are not allowed to. In order not be able to do that, the devils are also afflicted with complete blindness and consequently also with the greatest foolishness. And their assemblies look like the guarded institutions on this Earth, in which the fools and madmen are detained, so that they cannot harm other people.

From what has been said now, all of you can easily realize how things are with Satan and his devils.

4.4 Judas Iscariot

Judas Iscariot had a lot of enthusiasm, was completely active and could speak and present the lessons well, and as such he was chosen by Christ for a mission along with the other eleven because of the good and not the bad sides. But since he achieved more through his earnest hard work and through his ability of persuasion in the same time as the other eleven put together, he also began to pride himself more than he was.

When his arrogance came up against something, a secret anger gnawed at him more and more, and from day to day he became more closed and had a sharp eye on the other eleven disciples, in order to spot something that he could bring up before Jesus. But since such did not happen which could have served to cool his anger, in secret he became ever bitterer and searched all the more fervently for an opportunity to embarrass his brothers.

He was a greedy and money-loving person who often presented with all persuasion the possession of money as something highly necessary for earthly life, because the worldly rulers had introduced it to relieve the otherwise tiresome bartering.

Once he even said to the wise Nathanael, with whom he spoke the most, that Jesus obviously need no money for earthly life, for being equipped with divine omnipotence, one could get by without money anywhere. But people without this potential and without having the luck to be His disciples, would have to have money for the earthly life as well, including and necessarily the emperor himself, in order to pay his soldiers and other state officials.

Nathanael always corrected him, saying that money was nonetheless a great evil among the people, although it could also be the reason for many good things in the hand of a just person, like all earthly goods. But it would still contain evil in itself, because it could awake the greed of man greatly and most of all it could be the reason for vices and iniquities of all sorts, from great to small.

Judas Iscariot accepted this idea, but explained money nonetheless to be a necessary evil, just as the body is also a necessary evil for the soul. But when the soul uses the body wisely, the body is then also a temple of salvation, through which alone it can achieve eternal life and the true childhood of God.

Because of his persuasive ability he was able to find a so-called legal angel everywhere, and it was difficult to argue with him. But he went so far with his legal opinions that he even claimed that theft was justified in an emergency, like the Spartans and Cretans did, and blamed Moses for feeblemindedness because he declared every theft to be a clear sin. But he did not consider that even the permitted, most necessary theft in time leads man to the greatest laziness and no one would work and save any longer, if he knew that, if he had any reserves, it would soon be discovered and taken away by those in need. But if such a custom would be allowed to the people, what would happen then to love for one's neighbor or the recognition of God?!

Nathanael showed Judas quite well that his justification of theft did not correspond with his highly economical ambitions and that permitted theft would destroy even the most correct thrift. But then he came back again with his concealed cleverness and so there was nothing that could be done with him. Only when Jesus chastised him did he leave off his ideas for a time and gave in to secret better considerations.

Judas Iscariot was learned in the Scripture, and Jesus also knows about all his knowledge and experiences from other places, in which he exceeds by far all His other disciples. But to what advantage was that to him, if he traveled around with Him for almost two and a half years, mostly to watch Him closely in everything He did, to see if he could find something which is not according to the Scripture? Because of that, his hidden pride, which he therefore did still not give up, and also his selfishness and possible pursuit of profit was always nourished anew. That is why he stayed as he is, and he did not allow anyone to rebuke him completely and truthfully to improve his life, because he always said to himself: "What do you, poor and ignorant fishers want to teach me, while I am learned in the Scripture?"

In itself it is very good to be learned in the Scripture. But to God, someone who knows little about the Scripture but who lives and acts in faith according to it is much more dear than someone who is very learned in the Scripture, and who only criticizes the Scripture, who hardly and finally does not believe in it at all, and therefore does not live and act according to the Scripture, but only according to the advice of his worldly reason.

Once a person has blown up himself by the vanity of his great knowledge, is as blind in the Spirit as all those extremely wise Pharisees and scribes in Jerusalem. Even so much so that in bright daylight he cannot see the forest between the trees, thus who is still searching it, and while is standing in the middle of it, he asks: "Yes, but where is that forest that I sought and wanted to see?"

From a spiritual point of view, is it also not the same as with someone who asks in the middle of his life if he is really living, and out of what his life actually consists? Fool, your skin and your flesh and the outer world that is equal to you will of course not be able to tell you, because all that is in itself no life, but only a result of life. Go into your inner being by faith, by love, by humility, meekness and true self-denial, and become through that an independent life with the life from God in you, then you will experience that you are truly alive and what life is!

Indeed, why do people not search for gold in dead rocks? But on a spot where they have discovered traces of that metal, they penetrate into the deep of the mountains and gather great treasures therein. If people do this without fear and restraint, just to win earthly treasures which are dead as such, and which also bring death to a lot of people, then why are they not doing this in and with themselves, to win the gold of life that is hidden in them? They already have the clearest traces of the inner and true gold of life on their skin.

Once a person exists and lives, but who as an unripe fruit of life is still not aware why he exists and lives, should, in his works, stand in the light from God. By that he should strongly enlighten himself and warm himself in his heart, and then by that he will come to an inner liberation and true ripeness of life. Therein he will clearly be aware how and why he exists and lives, and what and who the life in him is.

5 Life and Death

5.1 In the beginning…

…God placed the Spirits as matured ideas, outside Himself and filled them with His power to such an extent, that they themselves become able to think and to will. They had to be shown the order on how they had to think, to will and finally to act. But with this given order, an impulse was placed in those first beings to ignore the given order; otherwise, they would never be able to make any use of their will. Only the impulse placed in them produced a true life emotion in them, according to which they began to decide, to chose, firmly to will and to act.

It is quite easy to understand that already in the first created spirits a certain weed had to begin to show, because the impulse lifted many of the first created spirits out of the order and finally by the continuously mightier growing opposition they had to harden, and in this way laid the foundation of the material creation of the worlds.

The first main central suns were created, and out of them finally all the countless other suns and world bodies and with them everything else what you can discover and find on, above and in them.

Everything what is now called matter was originally spiritual, which voluntary has stepped out of the good order of God, founded itself taking the wrong decisions and hardened therein, which then formed matter. Matter is therefore nothing else then out of itself hardened spirit under judgment; or stated more clearly, it is the most coarse and most heavy skin or shell of the spirit.

However, the spiritual can with all the still so hard and coarse surrounding shell never become so quickly complete matter, but continues to live and exist in matter, irrespective of its nature. If the matter is very hard, the spiritual life in it is also severely bound and cannot express itself or unfold any further, if it is not given any help from the outside.

In a hard rock life can only reach some expression, if the rock over a long time is soften and is getting more and more eroded by rain, snow, dew, hail, lightening and other elements. Thereby some life escapes as ether into the air, some part forms itself a new and lighter wrapping, initially in the form of tender mould or moss plants; but over time dissatisfied with this wrapping, the more freer life seizes each other and creates soon a new wrapping, wherein it can move more freely and independently.

As long as the new wrapping is tender and soft, the imprisoned spiritual is quite happy and does not asked for anything better. But in time the initial very tender wrapping becomes again harder and more coarse, by the inner activity of the spirits, which now increasingly pushes the pressing matter to the side; therefore the spiritual life strives upwards, hence forms the blade of the grass and subsequently the trunk of the tree and tries to protect itself from the below, following increasing hardening, by the continuously produced and increasingly narrower rings and incisions. But since in the end by this activity no rescue from total solidification can be expected, they narrow the lower trunk as much as possible and escape further into the small twigs, threads, leaves, and finally into the flower; but because eventual all this effort within a short time become harder and harder, the biggest part of the spirits recognize that all their efforts are in vain and they start to preserve themselves so to speak into cocoons, which they quite firmly surround them with corresponding better matter.

Thereby all kind of seeds and fruits originate. But the most selfish part of the freer life in a plant does not gain much; since that what enclosed itself in a firm germ shell, must complete the journey as many times as the seed gets into the moist and life saturated earth. The other more patient part of life, which allowed itself to become a guard and carrier in the lower matter for the most keen, most timorous and most impatient life, soon decays and passes over into an even higher and freer life sphere, still continues to wrap itself, but normally already with corresponding animal forms; and what has been consumed as fruit by animals and even people, the coarser part will be used for building and feeding the flesh, while the more noble part becomes nerve-strengthening and enlivened energy, and the very noble part becomes part of the soul substance.

5.2 *Life as it is!*

It is true that on this Earth life is perpetually exposed to all kinds of enemies and must always be ready to battle and to assert itself as life. However, this battle applies only to matter under judgment by the omnipotent will of God, which always has to suffer the most then, when its inner spiritual life, which we call soul, separates itself from the physical matter and rises to a superior level of life.

All the physical matter – from the hardest rock up to the ether high above you – is soul substance, in a limited and rigid state. Its destination is to return to an unbound, of a pure spiritual being, if it has reached, by this isolation, the necessary life independence. But to reach this continuously increasing self-activity, the soul freed from bound matter must go through all possible levels of life and must in each new level of life, wrap itself anew in a material body, from which the soul again attracts new life and activity substances and makes it her own.

Once a soul which is in a body (which her Spirit out of God can clearly see, being it the soul of a plant or that of an animal) by the necessary ripening has achieved the ability to rise to the next higher level of life, the soul's Spirit, which continuously is developing the soul in the beyond, arranges that her further unusable body is taken away from her, so that she then, already equipped with higher intelligence, can build for herself another body, wherein she again for a shorter or also longer period of time can work herself up to an even greater life and intelligence, and this process continues up to the human level, where she in this last body, as already totally free, could reach full self-consciousness, the recognition of God and Love, which we call the rebirth. If a human soul has reached this degree of life, she is perfected independent being and as such will not be destroyed and devoured anymore by the most general divine all-being and all-life.

The surest sign of the already attained life independence of a human soul is and consists therein, that she recognizes God and even loves Him with all her strength. For as long as a soul does not recognizes God as a being separated from herself, the soul is still blind and deaf and not free from the power of the divine almightiness; she then still has to fight immensely to free herself from such chains. But as soon as the soul begins to recognize the true God as outside herself and begins to properly perceiving Him intrinsic through the feeling of love, she then is already free from the bonds of divine almightiness and belongs then also already more and more to herself and is therefore self-creator of her own being and life and thereby an independent friend of God for all eternity.

Coming back to the fight the soul bear for its own development, a question arises: What is it about the body of this rabbit with which the eagle satisfies its hunger, at the same time freeing the soul of the little animal, so that it already has the full ability to rise to a higher level of life? The eagle also has a soul striving for the same destination. In the flesh and blood of the rabbit still exists more coarse soul substance. This will be united with the soul substance of the eagle so that the eagle's soul thereby becomes a little softer and more intelligent and after the loss of its body can already become something of a human soul, gifted with a considerable amount of light, courage and power.

This has been the way for growing up of the children of God on this Earth. Life is and stays a battle with all kinds of enemies for as long as it has struggling to become a winner over all matter out of its own power. And as such, one should not be surprised about all the material life enemies, since they are not enemies of the actual life, but only enemies of the material life. Actually, the latter is no life at all, but only a tool of the true, inner, spiritual soul life, and is the means whereby she can work her up to the ever increasing, truest actual life freedom, which would not be thinkable possible without this temporary cvasi-life.

God of course, with His almightiness, can produce a Spirit with perfect wisdom and power out of Himself, and this in one moment countless many. However, all such Spirits would not have independence, since their will and actions are nothing else than those of the Divine Self, which must uninterrupted flow into them, move and act through the Divine Will. For themselves they are absolutely nothing, but pure momentary thoughts and ideas of God.

However, in order to become independent in time, they must go the way of matter or the judged and thus fixed will of

God, in the manner as you have it before your eyes on this earth. If they have done this, only then they are independent, self-thinking and voluntary acting children of God, who indeed always do the will of God. And they are doing so not because it has been imposed on them, but because they recognize what is highly wise and decide by themselves to act accordingly, which is then for themselves life rewarding and provides for them life's highest bliss and happiness.

The higher degree of life of the soul takes place in the physical world, as well as in the dream, when the spirit in the soul becomes just as active as the spirit of a plant in the grain of seed, acting in the flesh of the grain to form and to let grow the roots in the soil and the little leaf germs above the soil. Then the soul begins to unfold to a real form and penetrates on the one hand in itself, just like the roots of a growing plant are penetrating into the soil and begin to suck in the right food from the godly power in it, while on the other hand the plant itself, thus fed from the inside – as a result of that inner feeding from the pure, true and living godly power – will in the sphere of light lift itself up and develop itself higher and further to the ultimate completion as the actual and real form of the being of the soul.

But all this happens by the continuously increasing activity of the Spirit in the soul, which by this will unite more and more with the soul. In this condition of the soul, his vision and intuition is no more a vague sensing but already a light and clear ones, becoming aware of all life conditions and of the relation in which they are to spiritualize his own life.

In this state of mind, man knows himself and also God and he can then also vision the spirits of respectively the souls of the already deceased ones as well as the still living people in the flesh and also see how they are. The visions of such a person will then not be material and unreal, but spiritual, pure, true and consequently real, and there will only be little difference between the clear seeing in an awakened condition and that of the bodily sleeping condition of a person.

There are certain devote people who are living and acting in the spirit world, almost daily, for the strengthening of their soul, during their bodily sleep. But when they wake up again, they do not know anything of it. They only perceive a kind of consoling, strengthening feeling in themselves and have the impression that they have heard and seen pleasant things.

Only those people who are as the prophets (on the transition to the third and thus highest and clearest degree of vision and feeling – because their Spirit is already more unified with the soul) are also bringing back to the awakened condition what they have seen and heard in the higher spirit world, and can say it also to their fellowmen. Most of the small prophets were in such a condition.

Look for instance at a stalk of corn, how it develops itself until in the highest point of its growth, when is developing itself as fruit. Look, the same thing happens with man, when the soul begins to pass completely into his Spirit.

By his activity, the spirit has begun to work on the still half material soul and has extended in her more and more, this as long as the whole soul has been filled by life and spiritually awakened to it. In the following stage, the soul, completely kindled by the love of the Spirit, begins to pass into the Spirit, and to change all her substance that is still related to matter into pure spiritual essence, and then the true fruit will be formed for the free eternal life.

In this condition, man is completely lifted up in the light, begins to be fed by it, and the more food he receives from it, the less food he will take from the substantial-material sphere of the soul, as an ever more spiritualized soul. The fruit of life blooms, thereby uniting itself with the spirit of love, and this produces again the grain of life, which at first is fed with the milk from the Heavens, but already after a short time with increasingly clearer and eternally firm and unwavering truths.

And look, then the grain of life becomes ripe, and the life of the soul, who in the second degree of vision – in a certain way unified with the spirit – is now in the completely ripe grain of life, and therefore the stalk that was so zealously formed before, withers, dies off completely, separates itself from the grain of life.

This is the highest degree of vision and life of the soul. In this condition the soul sees and hears everything there is in the whole of creation. He sees the Heaven opened and can have the most illuminated and living contact with the whole spirit world. What such a soul sees, hears and feels, can never more be removed from his very clear memory, for his extremely clear sphere of vision and feeling is all-embracing, eternally lasting and all-penetrating.

The great prophets were in such a condition, and also all completed spirits of the Heavens are in such a condition.

5.3   About nutrition

Whenever the soul demands material food for her body, she also therewith always receives a legion of liberated and still evil and impure spirits into her body, which then must aid her in the ongoing body-building process. The spirits gradually seize one another, soon forming their own souls, intelligent after their kind. After raising themselves to such level, they abandon the soul, as authorized possessor of the body, starting to make such arrangements within the body as will suit their imagined well being.

Once such spirits have reached a high degree of imagined well being (as is the case with rapacious souls within young bodies) then other phenomenon can and must make its appearance with such children. The foreign matter must be cast out through an appropriate illness, unless it is intended to let the child go through a virtual spirit possession; or, in order not to torment some weaker child's soul too much, one allows a soul to live wretchedly within such half-foreign body until a certain time, and then, through instruction either by the external or internal spirit world, to bring that soul to a level of insight where in the end will voluntarily starts to drive out her parasites, through fasting and all sorts of other self-depravations; or, where the parasites are too stubborn, one takes the whole body away, and then develops such a soul in another world, for eternal life.

Such cause also underlies the occasionally early physical death of the child, so bitter for the parents. Therefore, especially parents should be particularly concerned about their children obtaining the appropriate external food.

If the mother eats unclean foods, then the mother should not breast-feed the child but let it be breast fed by someone eating clean food, or she shall have much trouble with the child. For this reason, since Abraham, and mainly through Moses, the clean animals and fruits were prescribed to the Jews, and many of those who kept such commandments conscientiously, never had sick children and achieved ripe old age, dying from old age feebleness.

In the present time however, when one makes a grab for even the most exotic delicacies, no longer even thinking whether the food is clean or unclean, where in some lands almost anything is constantly stuffed into the body that is not either stone or clay, there it is in any case a wonder that blind mankind has not yet sunk back into the animal forms corresponding to what, surely, they already attained in their psyches.

If, currently, healthy born children in their first few years already are stricken with all kinds of maladies, then an obvious cause lies in the most inappropriate nutrition, through which a multitude of evil and unclean spirits are conveyed into the body, which not seldom has to be completely removed, for the good of the soul; and therefore nothing but inexcusable parental blindness alone is responsible for the early physical death of the child, because such parents would rather follow anything than the divine advice in the Holy Book.

Through His angels, God undertake an annual thinning out of all fruit trees, from whose fruits men feed upon and no apple, pear or fruit of any kind whatsoever must be eaten before ripen, because during flowering some unclean spirit could settled in up to the fruit stage. And such fruit is cast down from the tree while still unripe. Similar care is taken with all types of grains and plants destined for human consumption.

But blind man not only does not recognize this but, akin to a polyp, eats everything that seems a tidbit to him. No wonder that he soon gets sick, sluggish, toilsome, crippled and therefore miserable through and through!

Therefore, all varieties of so-called root plants are more than bad for children and breast-feeding nannies, as also for pregnant women, while coffee is still worse. But blindness sees nothing, avidly consuming both for the pleasant taste. And children get physically miserable, followed closely by their parents.

If man wants to stay completely healthy in body and soul, from childhood he must moderately nourish himself with pure food. Jesus Christ was also a human being, for what His soul and body are concerned, but he eat and drink always the same clean food and quench his thirst with pure, good and healthy wine, but always in the right measure. His family and most of his disciples were almost all fishermen and lived from fish. When they had a surplus of fish they caught, they received money, and with that they bought the necessary clothes, bread, salt and also wine which they drank in moderation with water, almost all of them was never tormented by a sickness.

If people would have stayed with the food that was indicated by the prophet Moses, the doctors with their medicines would almost never have had any work to do for them. But they began to stuff their body – just like the pagans in the manner of the epicures – with hundreds of different so-called delicacies and by that, after a short time, they fell into all kinds of sicknesses.

A good kind of fish that stays in clean water and that is prepared in a well manner is the healthiest food for the human body. Where such fishes cannot be found, wheat and barley bread are in itself the healthiest food for humans, as well as the milk from healthy cows, goats and sheep. Among other vegetables, lentils are in first place and also the big Persian maize grain. Only the flesh of a few chickens and doves, then of a healthy and clean bovine animal, and also of goats and sheep, in a completely bloodless condition, can be eaten as food – fried or cooked, but fried is to be preferred to cook. The blood of animals should not be eaten by anyone!

This is and remains for men the simplest, purest and healthiest food. All the rest – moreover when it is eaten in excess – is harmful for man, especially when it is not prepared in such a way that the evil of the nature spirits is completely removed from it.

How about the many kinds of very good tasting fruits and roots?

The eatable fruits must in the first place be completely ripe. In that condition they can be eaten with measure. But nevertheless, it is healthier when they are in a cooked, fried or dried form than raw, because by the boiling, frying and drying the bad and still unfermented nature spirits of life are removed from them. It is the same with roots.

Many fruits and roots are good for men's consumption. However, the hungry and gluttonous people will not be satisfied with that, but they constantly still discover a great number of things to eat, from the plant kingdom as well as from the animal kingdom, and the results of this are the ever increasing, most various physical sicknesses.

Besides that, you should be moderate in eating and drinking and not be eager for artificial delicacies, then you will keep the health of your body for a long time, and death will be as the pleasant falling asleep of a worker who became tired in the true vineyard of God. The soul will thereby float away happily and clear-sightedly from the bodily envelopment that has become frail, and will be lead into the indescribable happiness of the Heavens by many friends, and he will be endlessly happy and cheerful because he finally is delivered from this world and its misery.

What is more than moderation is evil for man. Excessive eating causes diseases of the stomach, but excessive drinking not only creates stomach and chest ailments but also lewdness and unchastity of every imaginable kind. Therefore, be moderate and sober in all things and you will have a healthy and cheerful soul in an always healthy body.

Whoever prepares food for him or others let him prepare it fresh and wholesome so that it will not harm him. In emergency, even a strict Jew can also eat the flesh of any animal, and it will serve well; for all nourishment that a person is forced to take in is purified by God – only he must observe an even greater moderation!

The flesh of pigs is good, but the slaughtered animal must bleed out and then be pickled for seven days in salt, vinegar and thyme and have a weight placed on top. It is then to be taken out of the brine, well dried with a linen cloth and hung for seven weeks in a smoke from good wood and herbs until it is completely dry and hard. Who then wants to eat it shall boil it at first in half water, half wine with the addition of thyme and parsley and will thus have a good and healthful food on his table. However, these animals must always be slaughtered in wintertime.

In the same way as the pigs also the other unclean animals must be handled if their flesh, eaten in moderation, is not to be harmful to man. What applies to the land animals also applies to the various species of birds of the air and the various animals in the great oceans.

Therefore, whoever will completely and entirely live and act according to Christ's teaching will also entirely be blessed with its happy results. But whoever will not do this completely and entirely, will also receive the blessing accordingly.

5.4 Cleansing the temple

The temple represents man in his natural-worldly sphere. In the temple, as also in man, there is the Holy of Holies. Therefore the exterior of the temple should be kept hallowed and pure so that the innermost, as the Holy of Holies of the temple as well as of man, may not be desecrated.

The Holy of Holies of the temple is covered by a thick curtain and only the high priest may on certain occasions enter the Holy of Holies by himself. The curtain and also the rarely allowed visit to the Holy of Holies is a protection against its desecration. For if someone sins with his body, he not only defiles his body, but also his soul and through it his spirit, which in every human being represents, and really is, the innermost and holiest life. This Holy of Holies in man, just as the same in correspondence in the temple, has been placed deeply behind a thick curtain, and only pure love for God, which in every man is God's truest high priest, is able to penetrate into this Holy of Holies. If, however, this sole high priest in man becomes defiled by attaching himself to impure worldly things, making common cause with them, how can the Holy of Holies remain undefiled if it is visited by an unclean high priest?

Therefore, if in the temple, as well as in man, everything has become unclean, man is no longer able to cleanse it, for if the broom is full of filth and dirt, how can it be used for cleaning? Then God Himself must take this work in His hands and cleanse the temple by force, and that through all kinds of painful experiences, like various illnesses and apparent accidents, so that the temple might be cleansed.

"Dealers" and "buyers" are the low, unclean passions in man, the cattle offered for sale represents the lowest animal sensuousness and at the same time also the resulting great foolishness and blindness of the soul, whose love may be compared to that of an ox that even lacks the sensual procreative and sexual love and is only motivated by the grossest polyp-like gluttonous love and whose cognition is equal to the well-known intellectual power of the sheep.

And what do the money-changers and their money dealings denote? They denote and represent in man all that emerges from man's already quite brutish self-love, for the animal loves only itself, and a wolf will devour another if he is hungry. These "money-changers", or such brutish self-love, must therefore also be painfully and forcefully removed from man, and everything that animates this love must be upset and scattered.

Why not completely destroyed? Because also this type of love must not be deprived of its freedom, for the noble seed or the grain of wheat will grow best in a field well fertilized with such dung and yield a rich harvest. If all the manure were removed from the field to cleanse it, as it were, from all the dirt, the grain of wheat would prosper only poorly and be sure to yield a very bad harvest. The dung which is initially carried onto the field in heaps has to be spread so that as to serve the field. If it were left lying in great heaps, it would suffocate everything where it is lying and be of no use to the other parts of the field. This is at the bottom of the story of the cleansing of the temple in the Gospel. And because of this reason Jesus only scattered the money of the money-changers and did not destroy it completely, which he could have done easily.

What about the pigeon-dealers inside the temple, who had to withdraw and return to the places originally allocated to them? They are to be understood as the external virtues consisting in all kinds of ceremony, custom, courtesy, etc, in a purely worldly sense which, however, men's blindness raises to an inner life value and tries to make true life to strike roots therein.

The pigeon is a creature of the air, and it was often used in the orient as a carrier of mail, especially in matters of love, and because of that in the ancient Egyptians its hieroglyph represents tender and nice conversation. It served as a symbol for such conversation in the temple and was at the same time an ordinary and correspondingly symbolic sacrificial creature. It was usually sacrificed in the temple by young married couples, when their first child had been born, as a sign that they now had done away with such external messages and passed into true, inner, life-giving love.

However, according to the order of all things, the outermost belongs to the outermost. The bark being something quite dead must never be contained in the marrow of the tree, but everything that belongs to the bark must also be deposited in the bark. The bark is most useful to the tree when in a proper measure in its rightful place. If someone would push the bark into the marrow of the tree, the tree would soon have to dry up and die.

And thus as an indication that men should not make external virtues a matter of inner life, whereby noble man would become no more than a conversation-puppet, these pigeon-dealers, in a broad sense all formalities, endeavoring to raise their merchandise to the status of inner life-values, were also expelled from the temple and ordered to their proper place, only in a somewhat gentler way.

So this is the spiritual meaning of the cleansing of the temple. And from the correct and unchangeable correspondence between man and temple, it can also be recognized that no man, but only God alone, as eternal wisdom, which sees and knows everything, can ever act and speak like this.

But why the Lord does not remain in the temple after such a sweeping? Because He alone knows what man's inner being must be like so that He may take up permanent residence in man. Besides, after such a cleansing, man must not be deprived of his freedom least he become a puppet.

Therefore, the Lord cannot yet entrust Himself to such a forcefully clean swept inner man, for He alone knows what is required for a full restoration of the inner man. That is why the sweeper walks out of the temple and, as if accidentally, flows from the outside into man's within, not submitting to man's request to stay with and within him which would only support man's indolence. Man has to awaken to complete spontaneity, thereby only becoming a perfect man.

5.5 *About sexuality*

Let's talk about this plague and annoyance called: lust of the flesh. Therein lays more or less the actual main evil for all people. From this lust originate nearly all bodily illnesses and most certainly and surely all evils of the soul.

Man can rid himself from every other sin easier than this; because the others have only outer motives, but this sin bears the motive in itself and in the sinful flesh. Therefore, you should draw your eyes away from the appealing dangers of the flesh for as long as you have not become masters over your flesh!

Keep the children from the first fall and preserve their innocence, and as adults they will easily control their flesh and not easily come to a fall; but only once overlooked – and the evil spirit of the flesh has taken possession of them! No devil is more difficult to be driven out of man than the flesh devil; only through a lot of fasting and praying can it be removed from man.

Beware to annoy the little ones or to stimulate them by excessive cleaning and stimulating clothes and to ignite their flesh! Woe to him, who sins against the nature of the little ones! Truly, for him it would be better, if had never been born! The sinner against the holy nature of the youth will be punished with all the might of God's wrath! Because if the flesh has become damaged once, the soul does not have any firm foundation anymore, and her perfection makes bad progress.

A great amount of work does it take for a soul to cure its damaged flesh and to make it completely without scars again! What fear does she not have to cope with, if she notices the damage and weakness of her flesh, her earthly home! Who carries the guilt of it? The bad supervision of the children and the many excitants, which are given to the children by all kind of things!

Above all is the depravity of moral standards in the cities, always greater than in the countryside; therefore, one should draw people's attention and show them the many bad consequences, which arise out of an too early break of the flesh, and many will take note of it, and many healthy souls will appear, in which the Spirit is easier to awake, as it is currently the case with so many!

Look at all the blind, the deaf, the cripples, the lepers, the gouty person; look further at all the different illnesses and with all kind of bodily illnesses afflicted children and adults! All are the result of a too early break of the flesh!

No man should touch a maiden before he is 24 years old, and the maiden should be fully 18 years of age; under this age she is only grow ripe and should not recognize a man. Because before that time she is only here and there grow ripe; if she is letting herself to be touched too early by a randy man, she is already a broken flesh and has become a weak and desirous soul.

It is difficult to cure the flesh, if she is broken before her time. The flesh will become from week to week more sexual, and finally become sex-addicted, which is a most wretched disgrace mark for mankind, not so much for itself, but much more for those, by which negligence they have become like that.

Woe to the one, who uses the poverty of another person to break her flesh! Truly, for that person it also would be better that he or she never had been born! Who has sex with an already spoilt person, instead of turning her away from destruction by using the right means and to help her on the right path, will one day have to cope with a repeatedly strict judgment before God; since someone hitting a healthy person, did not sin so severely, as someone who mistreated a cripple.

Who slept with a fully ripe and healthy maiden, has in fact also sinned; but since the caused evil is not of a particular harmful nature, especially if both parties are completely healthy, only a smaller judgment is placed on it.

A lusty person is in her flesh and her soul completely ruined and broken. Who is helping her out of such great distress with a reasonable and loyal heart, will one day be large in the Kingdom of God. Who sleeps with a whore for a pay and makes her even worse as she was before, will one day be rewarded with the reward that every willful killer receives in the mud pool, which is prepared for all devils and their servants.

Woe the country, woe the city, where prostitution is conducted, and woe the earth if this evil is getting out of control on her ground! Over such countries and cities God will place harsh laws which will burden the people with unreasonable loads, so that all flesh is starving and let go of this most sacrilegious activity, which one person can commit against his poor fellow people!

A whore will lose all honor and respect, even with those who have used her for a wage, and her flesh will in future become even more afflicted with all kind of incurable or at least difficult to cure. But if one betters herself properly, she will be looked with merciful eyes.

If any lecherous reaches for other satisfying means except the vessel which I have put in the lap of a woman, he will not easily reach the point to see the face of God. Indeed, Moses has ordered stoning for that, which Jesus does not completely repeal, because it is a hard punishment for similar offences and offenders who already have fallen to the devil. I only give you the fatherly advice, to ban such sinners from society, to expose them to severe distress in a place of exile, and only if they come, nearly completely naked, to the borders of their home country, to re-accept them, take them to a soul heal institution, which they should not leave, until such people have been completely rehabilitated. If they, many times tested for a longer period of time, are able to completely prove their betterment, they are allowed to return to society; but if the slightest signs of sensuous challenges are recognizable, they rather should stay imprisoned for the rest of their lives, which is many times better and healthier than the uncontaminated people in a society become contaminated by them.

On the other hand, in order to be fully chaste, should one totally suppress this most powerful of all natural impulses? But if that is so, then the marriage bed is certainly nothing more than a workplace for unchastity which is accepted in society; for who can guarantee us that the man does not sleep with his lush wife more often than is necessary to create a fruit?

I have seen and known people who one could call true people of gold as far as goodness, love, patience, kindness and compassion is concerned; but in the vexed question of chastity they were and remain weak. They did everything, it is true, to become stronger in this area, but it was not in their nature, not even when the natural, full impotence fell on them; a lush virgin still made the same lustful impression on them.

Also, I have seen and known people who remained as cold as a stone at the greatest female beauty, true examples of chastity, but otherwise in their lives they were insensitive to everything! Nothing moved them! Affliction and misery of the poor were laughable things for them, tears of suffering were tricks to wake sympathy; a woman was contemptible to them and very easy to do without, something which had no other purpose in the world than a field for the sowing of any kind of grain. They found marriage to be one of the most laughable institutions in human society. In their opinion all healthy women should be locked up in a great building and let strong men well capable of producing heirs sleep with them so that only beautiful, healthy and strong people would be created; but the ugly and weak women should be weeded out or used for the lowest jobs like cattle and work until they perish!

The answer for this dilemma is the following: if the life of a person is no flirting joke, but instead a very holy earnest, the sexual act can also be no flirtation, but also only a very sacred love act. The pleasant sensations of the act itself should not be the motive for the action. If you grasp this, you will soon find that the pleasant sensations are only accompaniments which facilitate the begetting of man in the nature of the flesh. If you are urged on by the reason of conception, then go and act and you will commit no sin. But there are nevertheless some points to be properly considered.

This act must not happen outside the sphere of true love for the other. The main reason for true love for the other is this: Do to others what you would have them do unto you!

Well, suppose you had a blossoming daughter who is a joy to your fatherly heart. You will care for nothing more than for the true happiness of your most beloved daughter. Your daughter may be mature and, therefore, capable of conception, but how would you feel if an otherwise healthy man came, driven by the urge to beget a child with a virgin, and by force begot a fruit with your daughter? You see, that would fill you with a fearful rage against such an offender, and you would never again let him out of your sight without the sharpest possible chastisement!

And nonetheless this person would have committed no sin against decency because he was seriously urged not to sow his seed outside a good vessel. But the act is nonetheless sinful, on the other hand, because true love was grossly violated!

You can see from this example, at such an otherwise very correct act not contradicting true chastity, must consider all other human side circumstances, if he does not want to sin against some law.

A a man can commit unchastity as well with his wife as with a whore and even worse. For with a whore there is nothing left to ruin, because everything has already been ruined anyway; but a wife can become overexcited and thereby run into a passionate desire, whereby she then can become a great sex-addict.

Whoever lays with a woman sins against chastity because his act only served – and had to serve – the gratification of mere lust but not the begetting of a human being, as pure reason must tell him that one does not sow wheat on a road.

Beside the sin against chastity, the one who lays with another one lover violates both his and her human nature, which again is a sin against the neighborly love.

5.6 *About death and the life in the beyond*

The cold reason shows you that you will die one day and what you are will pass away from this Earth forever; but on the other hand, ask your feelings and your perception and both of these will not know, and will not want to know, anything about the act of dying or passing away from this Earth.

Well, who is right and true – the cold reason, or the warm feeling of life? I tell you: Both, the reason and the warm self-perceptive feeling of life! Reason, as the ordered mental library of the soul, will clearly pass away from the soul, as well as the soul itself. Along with the other parts of the body and its limbs, its material capacity to perceive and calculate must also have the perception of passing away within it; but it is different with the feeling of life and with the being-aware-of-oneself, which, because it comes spiritually from God, has never had a beginning and therefore can also never have an end!

For this reason it is also impossible for the soul even in its material form to think of itself as temporary and ending. And so the soul becomes lighter and lighter, and if it is fully one with the spirit of God living in she, then the feeling of life becomes so clear and powerful that the feeling of temporality in the cold calculation of reason loses every meaning and power.

The reason for this is that all the life-force of the spirit of the Lord in the soul also penetrates even the spiritual nerves of the body and takes away every feeling of passing away. Finally, this occurs because at the end all the actual, ethereal bodily matter of life becomes immortal like the substance of life in the soul.

After a man dies, the soul is taken from the body and prevailing as an isolated spirit man, comes to a location corresponding to its complete living being; and here nothing will help it other than its free will and love. If the will and the love are good, then the location also will be good. The soul herself shall prepare it, in accordance with its God-implanted strength and authority. If the will and predilection are bad, then its effort also shall be bad – just as on earth a bad tree bears no good fruit and a good tree bears no bad fruit. Go and adorn a thorn bush with gold and precious stones and see whether it shall bear you grapes as a result! A vineyard shall bear sweet grapes full of flavor, whether you adorn it with gold or not.

If that is so and impossibly otherwise, ask yourselves what the whitewashing of graves, within which reside only decaying skeletons and obnoxious filth, should or could benefit the souls of the dead?

Do you earnestly believe that God is so feeble minded and vainly foolish that He should let Himself be served with the most vain and trivial parade of matter through matter?

God is a Spirit, and those who would serve Him must do so in spirit and fullest, living truth of their heart, but not in matter through matter, which is nothing but the transitorily shackled will of the almighty Father.

What actually means the death of man? Nothing else but the ripe fruit that falls from the tree and this falling off happens also by itself without special help of the fruit. When a person has matured in his inner being, so much so that he can be considered a ripe fruit, the releasing of the ripe soul from the trunk – the body – will also happen without any force. He who lived according to God's will, for him that moment will come in such a way that he will glide over from the earthly to the spiritual life, completely without pain, even with the most joyful feelings.

Despite that, one which is not really attached to divine life will have some kind of worry for that moment to come, and think that it will be the easiest to get over this unpleasant turning point if it is strengthened by God's presence. But one should lay down this forgivable human weakness because his faith, which kept him spiritually alive, will be more than enough, because the faith in God is actually the best and only way to conquer all threatening terrors of death.

Once man has become fully believing, and when God have laid into his heart that it is his time to loosen the bands of his flesh, because he finished his earthly task, God will even give him the power to break those bands himself, and then he will softly doze away in peace, before the eyes of those who are his own.

This is how death should be! This is rarely happening because most of men fear the moment that they are called away, more than anything else in their fearful life. As we know, usually their transition is not caused by the normal deterioration, but by violently destroying the physical machinery. The wrong life has therefore also brought about the many sicknesses, which should have nothing to do with the actual death, because not these sicknesses should determine the transition of the soul, but the complete ripeness of the soul.

When you will live in such a way that your soul will be completely reborn in his Spirit, that Spirit will quickly and easily be able to settle with all impure spirits that are still in your flesh, and then you will die a blissful death. But someone who generally will indeed seriously live and act according to the teaching, but besides that will still secretly fall back into his old habits, then he also will not be able to reach the complete rebirth of his soul in the Spirit, and finally during his passing away, with all humility and patience, he will have to accept that he still will have to struggle with many sorrows. Because that, the suffering will be the fire which will purify the life's gold of men from many dross. What is spiritually impure cannot enter Heaven, which is as much as saying the following: the pure Spirit out from God cannot unite completely with the soul, until this soul has completely and forever banned everything out of himself that belongs to matter and its judgment. Indeed, whoever wants to separate with a blissful bodily death from this world must take this well into account.

It goes without saying that here there can be no talk of an individual case, but only about the basic norm, according to which, during the guidance here and in particular also in the beyond, a soul is lifted out of the life-restraining physical state. In addition there are countless deviations, of which each is treated a little differently. But irrespective of all this, there must be a fundamental norm, according to which all the others must be directed. In a similar way, the earth must be fertilized by rain, so that in it the sowed germs can start to germinate. But how can the various types of seeds which are resting in the earth waiting to become alive, attract out of the raindrops the right substance, which is familiar to them? This is a matter of the specific intelligence of the spirits, who are residing inside the germs and know quite well how to provide for their residence.

According to this most necessary and unalterable life norm, if a so called poor and naked soul in the beyond immediately gets in contact with a spirit like for example Raphael, it would be immediately consumed by him, like the sea consumes a single drop of water. Therefore, care is taken by God throughout the whole of infinity, that a small, weak and still stupid-naked life is always kept in isolation, so that it exists individually as on its own and only such life potencies are allowed to come near it, which are not very much stronger than the individual life on its own, in its isolation and nakedness.

Such life potencies cannot consume each other, because they are of the same power and strength; but they still form associations and hold meetings, from which, however, never any good is forthcoming, because the wisdom of each separate being is exactly the same. Imaging a council consisting of a group of very silly people, who want to decide something quite wise and to execute it with combined forces! What will be forthcoming from their meetings? Nothing but silly stuff!

Even today we still have on this earth, and mainly on the islands, nations who are living undisturbed on their land since the times of Adam; they are descendants of Cain, who are still standing on the same cultural level, where they were standing thousands of years ago. Yes, why don't they have made any progress regarding their culture, but rather have moved backwards with all their many council meetings? Because the most wise among them was sillier and blinder than a stupid pig shepherd in this country! But if the wisest does not know anything, what should the others know, who are coming to him for advice?!

One of course can ask here and say: "Now then, why didn't God send any prophets who are filled with His Spirit to these nations?" With that we have come to the main point!

In these nations there still reside too unripe and naked souls. A higher revelation would consume them and would encapsulate them with a judgment, from which it would be almost impossible to free them. The highest and purest truth would transform them into the thickest superstition and they would bind themselves to such an extent to it, that in the end even God Himself by no means would be able to free them from it. Therefore, it is necessary that they stay as they are for another thousand years. Only after such time will they receive visits from pure mind awakened people, however, not to receive any lessons for quite some time, but only to obtain an awakening example. From time to time, they will be given quite often such awakening surprises. If this occurs for a few hundred years, then such naked nations will become somewhat more dressed, bodily and in the soul, and only then become in time ripe for a higher revelation.

And in exactly the same manner, and even more significantly troublesome, the development and life perfection of a naked nature soul progresses in the beyond. She must be left by herself in complete darkness for as long she is not pressed by her own suffering, to awaken herself out of her still partly material lethargy and starts to think about whatever more specific thoughts in her heart.

If the thoughts become an increasing distinctive and certain outline, a very faint dawn starts to appear in such a soul, and she starts to get a ground, on which she can stand a little and in time can walk around a little. This walking around corresponds with one thought passing over to the next and one emotion to another. This is a search, and a search must be followed by a finding, because otherwise the seeker, if for a too long time does not find anything, he finally will tire, because of his fruitless troubles and would fall back into his earlier lethargy.

But if the diligently searching soul starts to find something, it gives her a new and higher impulse for a further and more diligent search and inquest, and if she then find signs of a similar being like her own, she pursues this like a tracking dog and does not rest, until she has found something, which at least testifies of a close-by being similar to her.

By this increased searching she becomes riper and tries to satisfy her hunger with everything, what she, like coincidently, finds to cover her substantial soul body. Here and there she even finds something, no matter how meager, to fill her stomach and to satisfy her burning thirst. Since once a soul becomes properly passionate because of the inner, increasingly lively life-fire, she continuously finds more, for which a need arises in her soul.

The Spirit, who guides and leads such a soul, like from a certain distance, must take the greatest care that she only finds on the search path what furthers her life perfection. In time, she can also find a similar soul, who is pressed by the same needs, with whom she of course immediately starts to communicate, like two persons in this world who are pursued by one and the same fate. They mutually question each other, feel sorry for each other and in time council each other what they could do, to make their circumstances somewhat more tolerable. It goes without saying that the second soul must only ostensibly resembles the first soul, who only recently left full isolation; otherwise a blind would be given to anther blind as a guide, whereby only too easily both could fall into a pit, and could find themselves in a worse state as it was during the earlier period of isolation.

The perfected spirit person meeting with the young searching soul, must be careful not to show anything about his perfection, but must in the beginning be completely what the young soul is. If she laughs, he laughs with her; if she cries, he cries with her! Only if the soul becomes annoyed and complains and curses about her fate, the spirit does not comply, but always plays the indifferent one, who doesn't care whether it goes this or that way with him! If she doesn't want to go better, now, she has to stay like she is! Thereby, the young soul becomes more pliant and will be content with even a small advantage, which again, like by chance, will presents itself.

If such a soul has found a small place in the beyond, she is left there for as long she does not feel any desire to improve her fate; since such souls resemble such persons here, who are content with only a very small piece of land, which barely yields them enough, to make a scanty living. According to their desires they do not have a longing for anything higher and more perfect and better, and they are also not concerned by it. As long as they have something to eat and have a good rest, they already are very happy and forever does not wish to have anything better.

It is similar with a soul who has stepped out of her isolation and by her troubles is looked after in such a way, that she regards her circumstances as tolerable and is not further concerned by anything, yes, even has a fear and shies away from it, because she abhors everything which could bring her any form of trouble.

We now have provided for a soul in the beyond in such a way, that she for example has found employment with quite good people, who provide for her with what is necessary, or somewhere she got, or even better found, an abandoned property with a little house and a richly set fruit garden and a few goats with milk, perhaps even a male or female servant; the guiding spirit then for the time being has nothing else to do then leave such a soul unhindered with her property.

For some time he is leaving her, and pretends, as if he is going to search for something better, but returns and talks about having found something better, but this "better" is much more difficult to obtain, and it can only be earned by a lot of trouble and hard work! The soul then surely will inquire what this trouble and work is all about; and the guide will explain this to the questioning soul. If the soul feels inclined to it, he will lead her there; in the other case, he will leave her there, but he will make sure that the garden will continuously yield less and less, until in the end it will not even yield what is absolute necessary to survive!

This soul will now apply all diligence, to make the garden to deliver a greater yield; but the guide must not allow that the soul reaches her goal, but must make it happen that the soul must recognize the fruitlessness of her troubles and expresses the desire to give up the whole property and take on employment, where she, with surely not more trouble and work, can still be provided for.

If such a wish is sufficiently vividly expressed by the soul, she will be guided further and given employment with a lot of work. The guide will then leave her again with some excuse, as if he also found very hard but otherwise quite well endowed work at another location. The soul will now be given work, which she has to execute very precisely. It is said to her and impressed on her heart, that every mistake is punished with a cut of the negotiated wage, whereby a voluntary harder work above the requirements is substantially rewarded.

The soul now either will do what is required or even go more, or she will be unhappy about the work, will become sluggish and fall into even greater suffering. In the first case she will be elevated and placed in a freer and considerable more pleasant state, where she gets more to think and to feel about. In the second case the guide will leave her in significant suffering, let her return to her earlier meager property, to find a little but by far not what is enough.

After a while, when a state of urgent need occurred, the now already much better looking guide and already lord and owner of many properties, will come and ask the soul what came over her to neglect the good and prosperous looking job. The soul will now make excuses about the hard and too heavy work which is beyond her strength; but it then will be shown to her that her troubles and efforts on this most meager small plot is much greater and still there is no hope, to ever reach only the most necessary advantage.

In this manner a soul will be brought to recognition, will again take on a job and surely do more good than before. If she does well, soon she will be assisted to move forward, but she is still left with the feeling that she has not yet died bodily; since material souls do not feel this for quite some time and must be educated about this in a suitable manner. The news about that becomes only tolerable to her, once she, as a complete naked soul, has reach a soul-bodily firmness dressed in already good clothes. In such a firmer state they are able to receive smaller revelations, because the spirit germ starts to stir within them.

Once a soul has progressed so far and has recognized that she now lives in the spirit world and that her everlasting lot solely depends on her, the only right way of love to God and the neighbor will be shown to her, which she has to walk according to her absolutely free will and out of her completely free self-determination.

If this is shown to her, alongside what she in any case most certainly must achieve, the guide will leave her again and will only return if she most seriously calls for him in her heart. If she does not call him and she walks on the right path, she is left alone; if however, she deviated from it and went down a bad road, he will let her encounter a corresponding suffering. If she recognizes her misstep and wishes to see her guide, he comes and shows her the complete triviality of her efforts and endeavors.

If thereupon she expresses the wish to amend herself, she again is given employment, and if she fulfills her duties, she will be promoted again, but not as quickly as the first time, since she could easily fall back into her old, material lethargy, from which it will be much more difficult to free her than the very first time, because with every relapse she hardens more and more, like a growing tree, and from year to year becomes more difficult to bend than during the early growth periods.

I tell you this, so that you should recognize how difficult and troublesome the progress is in the beyond regarding the perfection of the inner life, and how easy and unrestricted it is here, where the soul still has the material body around herself, where she can foremost deposit all her present physical state, how and whenever she wants to do this. In the beyond this is not so easily possible, because the soul does not have a material body anymore and cannot glide with her feet over a material earth, but only over a spiritual one, which is built out of the thoughts and ideas of the soul, and which is certainly not suitable to adsorb and bury forever the physical state which has been expelled by the soul.

Whatever falls from the soul onto her earth is nearly the same as taking a stone and hurling it away from this earth into infinite space. Yes, who would possess the strength to hurl a stone with such speed-power up or away from this earth, to exceed the speed of a shot arrow by thirty-thousand times, would most likely be able to remove the stone so far away from earth, that it never falls back again; but any lesser speed-power would never manage such effect. It would drive the stone more or less far from earth; but if the throw-power becomes necessary weaker due to the gravity power of the earth, the stone eventually would turn around and fall back onto the surface of the earth.

And see, similar it stands with the material sin lumps still attached to the soul in the beyond! Even if the soul removes them from herself and throws them onto the surface of her world, the trouble is of little use to her, because the surface of the soul, on which she stands and moves in the spiritual world, forms very much part of her, like in the physical world the gravity of this earth, which forms part of this very earth, nevertheless how far out reaching it is, it will not allow even one atom to be remove from it.

If the soul in the beyond wants to get rid of everything coarse and physical, a higher power must become active inside her; and this is the power which lays in the Word! Since it is written, coming out of the mouth of God: "Before Your Name all knees will bend in heaven, on earth and underneath the earth!" Since only to this earth the high privilege is given, it implies its worthiness is standing above all other worldly bodies; they are therefore standing morally underneath this earth and hence also their inhabitants, by which must be understood "who are living underneath the earth".

Therefore, through God's Word the soul can completely be purified. But this cannot be done so easily in the beyond as one might imagine; it takes large preparations and efforts! The soul must in advanced be practiced in all possible self-activity and must carry quite a substantial strength firmly in herself, before it is possible for her to accept God's Word.

Once the soul is able to do this, it will be easy for her to remove even the last material atom from her entire territory to such an extent, so that it forever cannot fall back again.

5.7 *About re-incarnation*

The life of a person's soul after the shedding of the body is, as is very easy to understand, a continuing progression, since the completion of the soul cannot possibly be the work of one instant. That is the reason why the soul is a being limited spatially as well as temporally and in a way forced into the certain beautiful human form like its previous material body. Therefore, according to space and time as well as to the very most unlimited power of the Spirit of God and His works, the soul can only gradually take in and understand infinity and eternity.

Now, it comes down to the standpoint of inner breeding, in which a soul left its body. If this has followed any existing good laws, the otherworldly condition of the soul will certainly be such that it can immediately set out for a higher level of perfection of the free life and always and always progress to a higher level.

But if the soul has had to leave the body either out of a lack of education or in the worst case for a lack of any good will at otherwise good familiarity with the existing laws, without previously having turned even a little towards the true and better in the physical life and its circumstances, well, then it will be very easy to understand for anybody that such a very weak, miserable soul will have to be placed on the other side into such a certainly not enviable position in which it will be purified and healed according to the highest love and wisdom of God from its animal crudeness and with time may rise to a higher level of life, from which it will then go easier to an even higher level.

It is obvious that the spiritual man, who develops himself only imperfectly in the earthly life because his heavy body is a big burden to him, must continue to live, for nobody will claim in himself that he can reach a perfection in this short earthly life that can bring him already very close to God. He has to deal with various obstacles in his body and with temptations of all kinds, so that his character will be hardened and his will be trained to do and to attract more and more what is good and remove the bad tendencies out of himself.

Once in the beyond, he will come into a new world which will ever more reveal to him the wonders of God and the universe where he will be able to see with his spiritual eye and not with his weak physical eyes that only show him the material world. While looking at the great works of wonders he now understands that the real bliss can only be found in the activity, and that God Himself is the most active Being. According to his progress, a suitable working sphere can be given to him that he zealously takes at heart. And in this activity and at the sight of his useful work he will experience true joy and the highest bliss.

Everybody has heard about a migration of souls. The faraway Orient still today believes very firmly in it. However, such believe has become very tainted, because they let the human souls return to the animal flesh. Alone, this is far from true!

That a human soul of this world collects itself out of the mineral, plant and animal kingdom and pushes upwards to become a human soul, has been shown to you to the biggest part and also how this takes place in a well arranged order. However, not even an incomplete human soul can ever migrate backwards anymore, except in the spiritual middle kingdom, according to the outer appearance, for the purpose of its humiliation and possible emerging betterment. If such has occurred to a certain degree, above which it cannot go any further due to a lack of higher abilities, such a soul can enter in a simply creaturely bliss on any other world body, which means going in its spiritual sphere, or, if she wants to, once again enter the flesh of this earth, a path along which she can attain higher abilities, which help her to attain the childhood of God. Thus also from other worlds souls migrate into the flesh of people on this planet, in order to attain those countless many spiritual properties, which are necessary to attain the true childhood of God.

Since this Earth is such a schoolhouse, it is treated by God with so much patience, leniency and forbearance. Who from you can comprehend this, comprehend also that you should keep it for yourself, since it is not given to all to understand all the secrets of the Kingdom of God!

To reveal to people too much about such extraordinary secrets has either no value at all or just very little; since firstly they cannot grasp it and secondly for them incomprehensible information can quite easily disturb their faith which at least they has acquired so far. To comprehend this in the true, inner, spiritual life depth takes obviously more than just the dead letter of the law and the prophets.

If one have to speak, one would have to speak with you for a long time in order to reveal the true purpose of the existence of all types of creatures. Only in general one can say to you this much, that everything that is visible and tangible for man is spirit under judgment and has the determination to finally cross over into a free and independent life, after assuming a long row of all sorts of forms.

The forms already begin right from stone through all the mineral kingdom, going up to the plant kingdom, through the whole plant kingdom to the animal kingdom and trough this to man, all are containers who take in life from God.

Every form corresponds to certain intelligence. The simpler the form, the simpler and lesser is its indwelling intelligence. But the more developed and complex a form, the more intelligence you will find in it.

Take for instance a earthworm and you will easily see from its activity that its very limited life intelligence is quite in conformity with its form; whereas, if you look at the already quite complicated form of a bee, by that you will find a much higher intelligence in the life form of this little animal. And so the intelligence increases up to man.

Since these forms are only temporary receptacles and bearers of a more and more consolidating and constantly increasing intelligent life, and since this continually ascending life leaves the earlier forms, according to measure and relation of greater unification of earlier simpler life-intelligences, it is certainly unimportant what happens in future to the lifeless form, which has been nothing else but an organic mechanism, properly furnished shell for the purpose of the indwelling life intelligence. It does not make any difference to the great plan of the Creator whether these fishes are eaten by us or by other animals, because the ultimate purpose of life will nevertheless be unavoidably attained.

It is well known that the lifeless shells still contain some nutriment, and by the mutual devouring of the lifeless forms also what is nobler passes into another life, and so you see here on this earth through the whole large chain of created beings a continuous struggle and an interchange of life up to man.

Even man's outer form, meaning his body is of any value only as long as it is occupied by the soul, which alone is alive. Once the soul has matured, it leaves this body forever and the body is consumed. It does not matter by whom or by what. Whatever life is in the body it belongs to the soul, and it is given back to the soul. Everything else passes as nourishment into a thousand other created life forms.

The Romans, the Greeks and the Phoenicians and also the Egyptians believed in the migration of the soul, and still believe in it today, just like the Persians, Indians, on the other side of the high mountains, in the vast, big and far Orient, and another large people, that live further to the east on big islands that are surrounded by the greatest sea of this Earth – and also still many other tribes on the vast Earth. But the truth, which was very well known by the first fathers of the Earth, is distorted everywhere and completely wrong.

They were teachers at first, but later came the priests full of greediness and lust for power. Because the true facts about the migration of the souls would not yield any offerings and interest to them, and that is why they let the human souls migrate again in the animals and let them suffer in those animals, out of which suffering only the priests could deliver them in return of great offerings.

6　The Method

6.1　The Teaching

The true and godly valid spiritual path consists of the following:
- Firstly, firmly and without doubt believe in the only one true God, who created Heaven and Earth and all that is in it;
- Secondly, love God and by faith recognized Him above all and live and act according to His will;
- Thirdly, love your fellowman as yourself.

To love God above everything means to recognize God and His revealed will and then act accordingly, out of true inner love, and for God's sake behave towards every other person as every reasonable person behaves towards himself; naturally we are speaking here about the pure love, as unselfish as possible, both towards God as well as towards every neighbor.

As everything good wants to be loved purely because it is good and therefore true, God also wants to be loved because He is highly good and highly true! But your neighbor must likewise be loved because he is the reflection of God, just as you are, and just as you he carries a divine spirit in himself.

That is the actual core of Christianity and it is easy to observe, much easier than the thousand laws of the temple which are mostly filled with the exploitation of its servants.

Through the exact observance of this teaching, the Spirit bound within a person will become freer and freer, it grows and finally penetrates the whole person and pulls into its life everything that is a life of God and therefore must last eternally, and in the highest possible holiness as well! But every person who is in a certain way reborn in his Spirit will never see death, neither feel or taste it, and the freedom from his flesh will be the greatest bliss to him.

For the Spirit of a person, fully one with his soul resembles a person in prison, through whose narrow light hole he can look out onto the beautiful surface of the Earth and see how free people cheer themselves with all sorts of useful occupations, while he must still languish in prison. But how glad he will be if the prison keeper comes, opens the door, frees him from all shackles and says to him: "Friend, you are free from every further punishment, go now and enjoy full freedom!"

The Spirit of a person resembles the embryo in the egg: once it has become mature through incubation inside the hard shell binding its free life, it breaks through the shell and enjoys its free life.

Man can achieve such things only through the exact and honest observance of the teaching which the Savior of Nazareth announces to the people. Now man, if he is reborn in the spirit he also receives other perfections, which simple natural fleshly people cannot imagine.

The spirit is a power in itself, like the divine one; whatever such a perfected spirit in a person wants, that will happen and must happen because there can be no other power and might in the whole of God's infinity, except for the life force of the spirit!

Whoever lives according to his self-esteem, which is usually saturated with self-love and pride, and cannot from all his heart forgive and bless ten times more the one who offended him in some way, will sooner or later have to taste the inevitable consequences of hostility against which he can by no means expect any protection from God, unless he has paid his debt to his enemy to the last penny. Therefore, do live in peace and unity with everyone! It is better for you to suffer an injustice than to do even an apparent justice to someone. Thus you will not educate avengers for yourselves, and the spirits, who otherwise would have become your enemies, will then be your guardian angels and ward off many a calamity threatening you.

He, who fully absorbs the Word and unfailingly acts and lives according to it, thereby absorbs God with all God's love, wisdom, might and power and has thus become a true child of God, from whom the Father in Heaven will not withhold anything He has.

The Holy Father cannot do anything more than reveal Himself in the person Christ, His Son, making of you, created beings under judgment, absolutely free gods and calling you His friends and brothers. Do consider what you are receiving with this revelation, and then the material world will no longer tempt you and you will easily overcome it. This is all the more necessary since you cannot become children of the Father in Heaven unless you have completely conquered the world within yourselves.

I do not intend thereby to make of you condemners of the world, but only wise users of it. Would you not call him a fool one who became so attached to some well serviceable tool he needs for his trade, that he does not want to use it for the purpose for which it is intended, but only keeps gaping at it with intense pleasure, keeping it in a cabinet to prevent it from rusting and thereby becoming less beautiful which would lessen his empty pleasure in it?

The world is also a tool for you with which, if appropriately used, you could produce much that is good and magnificent. But being Christ's disciples you must use this tool in the way Christ has taught you.

Used and applied thus, this tool will prepare and secure for you eternal life, but if you use it in a different way, this tool will become like a very sharp knife in the hands of small children who could only too easily deal themselves a deadly wound with it which hardly any doctor will be able to heal.

Receive also Christ's full blessing with these words and do pass them on to all those who have not been able to hear them, so that in the end no one will be able to plead ignorance of Christ's teaching.

Christ task and teaching consist simply in showing man where he really came from and what he is, and in pointing out his destiny which will be fulfilled in accordance with the fullest and most evident truth.

Already the Greek sages said: "The most difficult, important and highest knowledge is the greatest possible degree of self-knowledge!" And exactly this is Christ's concern, for without this cognition it is impossible to recognize a Supreme Deity as the cause of all coming into existence, being and permanency.

Whoever does not recognize this and does not direct his life, his senses and striving towards this one true purpose in life, in order to recognize in himself the Spirit as a part of the Supreme Deity, the Eternal First Cause of all being, is as good as lost. The man, who is not fully at one with and within himself with God, is like a thing devoid of the inner, incessantly growing, more and more consolidating within, and soon disintegrates.

Man can achieve this by fully recognizing God as his first cause and then, in accordance with such knowledge, becoming active in his whole life-sphere. Once a man has reached this maturity and consistency within himself, he has also become a master over all the forces emanating from God and, through these, spiritually and materially also a lord over all creatures and is then in and for himself no longer destructible through any force and, thus, has gained eternal life.

That is the summary of Christ's whole new teaching, which however, in the basis of basics, is actually the very oldest teaching since the beginning of man on this Earth! It has only been lost through the idleness of humanity and is now given as if new again by Christ as the lost original Eden (Ye den = it is day) to the people who have a good will.

Christian teaching consists in short therein, that man should recognizes God and loves Him above all and loves his neighbor, irrespective what and who he is, high or low, poor or rich, male or female, young or old, just as himself. Who does this all the time and avoids sin, will soon experience it in himself, that such teaching is truly from God and has not come out of the mouth of a person, but out of the mouth of God; since no person could know what he should do, to attain the everlasting life, and in what this consists. Only God knows this and in the end also him, who heard it from the mouth of God.

All people who want to reach the eternal life must be taught by God; those who only hear it from people are still far away from the kingdom of God. They hear the words slipping from a mortal tongue, and like the tongue which gave the words is mortal, it is the same with the word in the person who heard it. He does not pay attention to it and does not make it alive by deeds. But the word coming from the mouth of God is not dead but alive, moves the heart and will of a person to the deed and thereby the whole person becomes alive.

But once a person has become alive by the word of God, that person stays alive and free for ever and will not ever feel or taste death – even by dying for thousand times through his body!

One will experience this after the Holy Spirit has come over one and will lead one into all truth! This will be the spirit of love, the Father Himself, who will draw and teach one, so that all can come there, where Christ is.

Nobody will come to Christ, if the Father is not open towards him! You must all be taught by the Father, thus by the everlasting love in God, if you want to come to Christ! Therefore, you all must be perfect, like the Father in heaven is perfect! Hence, a lot of knowledge, also the most plentiful experience will not bring you there, but only the living love for God and in the same measure to your neighbor; therein lays the great secret of the rebirth of your spirit out of God, in God.

However, everybody will have to walk with Christ through the narrow gate of the fullest abnegation, until he or she becomes what He is. Everybody must cease to be something for himself, so that he can become everything in God.

To love God above all, means: to completely rise and become one with God! To love your neighbor also means: to completely know and understand your neighbor, otherwise one will not be able to love him completely; because a partial love is of no use for one who loves, nor to one who is loved.

If one wants to have a full view in all directions from a high mountain, one must climb to the highest peak; because from any lower vantage point a considerable section will always remain concealed. Therefore, in love everything must occur from within, so that its fruit can be revealed.

Man heart is a field, and the active love therein is the living seed kernel; your poor neighbors are the fertilizer. Those of you, who will place many seed kernels into the well fertilized ground, will also reap a full harvest. The more you will fertilize the ground with your love for the poor, the stronger it will become; and the more you place good seed kernels into it, the richer the harvest. Who will sow plentiful, will also harvest plentiful; who will sow sparsely, will also harvest sparsely!

Therein lays the highest wisdom, that you will not become wise without the liveliest love. Therefore, all knowledge is of no use without love! Therefore, do not strive too much for a lot of knowledge, but rather that you love a lot, then love will give to you what no knowledge ever can give to you!

But again, love is a result of the stimulation of the inner life which has been acted on by something. The inner life is love, thus a fire possessing warmth. This fire is nourished if acted upon by a thing which itself has fire within, as the fire in the hearth is nourished by good firewood; it will begin to burn more vigorously, and there will be more stirred-up vital warmth from the inflammable substance. Thus, the flames will grow stronger and their light brighter, and the soul will soon obtain much light on a matter previously quite unknown to it. Thereby the love will keep growing, and it will not give it up until it has become thoroughly familiar and fully aware of its worth and all it contains. But this happens only when the love for the object keeps getting greater and more intense.

However, if the life is not stimulated by something, it remains cool and is not in the least interested in the ever so memorable thing, just as the flame does not lick at the logs of wood which are too far removed.

Therefore, before man can think living thoughts of warmth about something, he must be stimulated by it. The cold truth, being a glimmer of the remote stars, can never arouse the inner life, because its inner warmth is thereby not increased, but diminished.

Up till now you have only searched with the icy-cold intellect, the lever to your search being your equally cold reason which accepted nothing as truth unless it could somehow be perceived through one of the senses.

Without love, all knowledge would be of little use for your souls. If in the future, you will sacrifice time to love your neighbor, then only one day will be of greater use for your souls. What use is it to be before Christ, if you nearly dissolve yourself because of amazement about His power, greatness and never fathomable magnificence, but outside your house are crying poor brothers and sisters of hunger, thirst and coldness! How wretchedly would sound and to no use would be a loud cheering and praising for the honor and glory of God, if you cannot hear the hardship of a poor brother! To what use are all the rich and most magnificent sacrifices in the temple, if in front of your door a poor brother perishes of hunger?

Therefore, your search should especially be directed towards your poor brothers and sisters; to them bring help and consolation! And you will find in a brother, who was helped by you, more than having travelled to all the stars and have praised God with tongues of Seraphim!

All angles, all heavens and all worlds with all their wisdom, cannot give you in eternity, what you can achieve, if you truly have helped a poor brother, who was in misery, with all your strength and all your means! Nothing stands higher and closer to God than true, active love!

If you pray to God, and while you are praying you don't hear the complaining voice of your poor brother who came to you for help, during your hour of prayer, then your futile chatter is damned! Since God honor exists in love – and not in the futile twaddle of your mouth!

The only true prayer in the spirit appealing to God does not consist in the movement of the tongue and the lips, but only in the active exercising of love. What use is it to you if you have decorated the grave of a prophet with many pounds of gold, but failed to hear the voice of a suffering brother?!

As it is said before, Christ's teaching can be very briefly summarized: love God above everything and love your neighbor as you love yourself. Without the true and living believe in a sole and everlasting true God, no person can attain life's mastership. Therefore it is above all necessary to believe in a true God; since for as long as one does not believe that there exist a sole true God, one cannot awaken any love for Him in its heart. Without such love it is impossible to come closer to God and finally become one with Him. Without that there can be hardly any talk of a true mastership of life, as someone wanting to become a master player of the harp, who never has heard anything about it and even less so has seen one anywhere.

For as long as you still ask and say: "Yes, where is this God and how does He look like?" - I say to you, that nobody can see the actual God being and live at the same time, since it is infinite and therefore also ubiquitously and as such is a pure-spiritual also the most inner substance of everything, in its effectuating will-power-light; in Himself and for Himself however, God is a person and lives in an inaccessible light which in the world of the spirits is called the Sun of Mercy. This sun of mercy however is not God Himself, but is only the effectuation of His love and wisdom.

Just as you can see the effectuation of the sun of this world thereby that it is present everywhere by its continual outflow of light to all conceivable directions, also the everywhere effectuating power of the Sun of Mercy effectuates as an out flowing light in all beings and is animating and creatively present.

Who now understands to accept and to collect as much light as possible from the Mercy Sun of Heaven in the heart of his soul and then to keep it through the power of love to God, creates in himself a mercy-sun which entirely resembles the primordial mercy-sun in everything, and the full inner possession of such mercy-sun is then just as much as the inner possession of the only true mastership of life.

You will recognize the clarity and the bright fullness of this most true teaching only if you have attained the mastership of life. The attainment of the full mastership of life is certainly no easy work, since it means a lot of observance, a lot of experience, a lot of thinking, will-power and acting accordingly.

Christ specifically has come into this world, in the person of Jesus, to teach us the greatest and most important art, without any compensation. Who accepts this, believes and decisively lives, does and acts accordingly, will infallibly attain the secret of life and will after the attained real rebirth of his own life's spirit in himself, become a master of his life and thereby also a master of the life of his fellow-men, because he will be able to show them the way to it and through mastering his own life he will be able to show them the great life's advantages of such mastering.

But nobody will become a master overnight and that the pure, even most solid knowledge about the means and ways for attaining this greatest art are absolutely of no use to any person, if he does not applies it fully practical to his life. The theory on its own is there of no use at all, but only the praxis.

It is similar with the learning of other arts. For example, if you want to learn how to play a music instrument masterly, like the Greek perfect lyre, or the even better sounding harp of the Jews, you have to engage a master of this instrument. He would teach you very precisely the rules which are absolutely necessary to play the music instrument, so that you precisely would know what you had to do and to practice to become in time a master musician yourself. Would you be already a harp, or lyre player with only the so precise knowledge of all rules, means and ways? O, surly not! You first had to troublesome learn the ability by diligently exercising the fingers and ears according to the rules known to you to become a master. And it is precisely the same with the attainment of the art of living.

Only by practicing one becomes a master, and the higher or lesser degree of the attained mastership depends directly on the greater or lesser practicing of the recognized rules. The more practice, the more the mastership! Therefore, you should not think that by the knowledge of the rules of life's art alone, you are already able to achieve something! Through pure recognition alone, you will not even nearly understand the possibilities, but by practicing such rules the veil of the Isis could be lifted! Only by continuous and diligent practicing you will come to the increasingly brighter realization, that the rules are right and true and will lead to the set goal. And once you have reached mastership through practicing, only then you will have totally lifted the veil of Isis in front of you!

6.2   *Love God above all!*

How can one achieve to love the all mighty God, the invisible, eternal Spirit, above all? For it seems the heart of man is too small and incapable of loving beyond measure the infinite and eternal Spirit of God, whom one cannot possibly imagine. It is easier to love one's neighbor; but to love God who is so misterious is certainly an extremely difficult matter for us, insignificant men. What must one do if one wants to love God above all?

Actually, nothing could be easier in the whole world. Let man contemplate the works of God, His goodness and wisdom, and conscientiously keep His commandments, let him love his poor neighbor as himself, and he will thereby achieve to love God above all.

However, if you are unable to form a concept of God touching your heart, look at Christ, and you will have before you that forever valid and lasting form which alone will portray to you your God the Creator. For God is also a Man, but the eternally Most Perfect One, both in and out of Himself. If you see Christ, you see everything!

Wherever a man has truly worked for the salvation of his soul, there and then he has performed the greatest work in a true and most unselfish manner. For a true activity serving the benefit and salvation of one's own soul totally precludes all other self-seeking activity anyway, because selfishness and self-love completely block the love for God and for the neighbor.

Whoever cares materially for his body seeks the treasures of this world, burrows in matter and thus buries his soul in judgment and in death! Even if such a man had worked all day long in the field, using plough and hoe with such diligence that by evening he is drenched in his own sweat, in His eyes he was nevertheless an idler and a lazy servant for the field of the Kingdom of God.

For, whoever does not work in the right and proper spirit within God's order for the true goal set for him by God, surely does not work for the temporal and eternal benefit of his neighbor either, and he does not deem it worth the effort to seek and more closely recognize God. A person who makes no effort to find and truly recognize God is even less inclined to exert himself for the benefit of his neighbor; and if he does something for him he does it only for his own sake, hoping that the neighbor might be able to return the favor several times over.

Who truly loves God the Lord is continuously with God and in God. And if he wants to hear or know something from God, he must ask Him in his heart, and through the thoughts of the heart he will immediately receive the fullest answer, and in such a way every person can always in all things be taught by God. Therefore, to be blessed in the Lord it is not always necessary to see, but only to hear and to feel – and you have everything what is required to be truly blessed in God.

6.3 About freedom

All egoists and those craving power are living proofs that life's highest bliss consists in the very possession of unfettered freedom of will and its most successful actual effectiveness. Who would hate crown, throne and scepter, particularly if he can attain them himself?

What gives these three effective rulers such an immense value in men's eyes? The answer is quite obvious and to the point: Because the one sitting on the throne make the freest and in the world most effective use of his will among millions of people.

But next to the one sitting on the throne, everyone appointed to some office by the ruler will be immensely happy, because he can, even though only in the name of the ruler, play at being a lesser ruler and give a little more rein to his freedom-loving will. To be sure, he vigorously suppresses his own absolutely free will, substituting it with the ruler's will, even though in his own mind he often does not agree with it; but all this he does so that he can also rule a little and make his will effective in some way. High government officials find now and again occasion to exercise their own free will, and this is for man sublime bliss already on this earth.

Yet, how could this be compared to that bliss which will, and must, result for all infinity and eternity from the merging of the human will, which is here always very limited, with the will of God?

You will understand that, before this can happen, the human will must be seriously developed – through the wisest guidance – in all stages of life, as otherwise it would certainly be exceedingly dangerous to endow man's free will with effective and absolute power.

In order to enable man's will to achieve this, one has to make sure that man will spontaneously enter the path of light, following it with all love and self-denial, until he has reached the right goal through his own actions and full self-determination. This can be achieved neither through an outer nor an inner compulsion, each of which is a judgment through which no human spirit can ever become free as far as his will is concerned; but as long as he cannot do that, there is not a chance of uniting his will with the freest will in God.

It is, therefore, necessary to lead the people solely through the wisest instruction into the true cognition of self and of the only true Deity, and this with all possible kindness, patience and gentleness. Only stubborn, unruly characters, which are secretly possessed by a senseless, evil wantonness and a truly devilish malicious pleasure, must be routed through an external worldly judgment, but they must on no account be punished too soon through some miraculous act.

At the same time, it must always be deeply considered that the one to be punished is also a human being who is to be guided to a proper use of his free will, and that possibly a cunning and revengeful demon may have gained control over his body, thus turning the otherwise perhaps quite harmless man into a veritable monster.

Therefore, any zeal carried to excess, even in the worthiest cause, must be restrained until that modest maturity has been reached which strives with all available means to set to work quietly and with loving care and wisdom, taking everything into account, always considering the living subject it has to deal with, in all its circumstances and stages of development.

It is exactly for this reason that Christ came to this Earth, in order to free all of us from the bands of creative necessity and to show us the way to true, independent, eternal freedom of life through word and deed and to pave the way and to smooth it through His example.

For as a man He is a human being like us; but within Him lives the original fullness of the divine magnificence of the Father, who is pure love. This is the will of the Father, that everyone who believes in Christ should have eternal life and the magnificence of the Father in him, in order to become true children of the Almighty and to remain so for eternity!

But in order to achieve this, heaven and hell must come together in this world! There is no victory without a battle! Where the highest thing is to be achieved, the highest activity must be fully undertaken to achieve it; in order to reach one extreme, one must first break away from the opposite extreme.

But how could a highest level be conceivable without the lowest?! Or can someone among you think of mountains without the valleys between them?! Are the summits of the mountains not measured according to the greatest depth of a valley?! Therefore, there must be very deep valleys, and whoever lives in the depth of the valley must climb up the mountain, fighting with many obstacles, in order to win the freest and furthest view. But if there were no valleys, there would also be no mountains, and no-one could climb any height with a view which only reaches a little over what is usual.

That is only a material parable, it is true, but nonetheless things which are similar and correspond to the infinitely great spiritual truth are hidden in it – for him who can and will think, things will constantly form themselves more significantly.

However, in the sphere of our soul, the inner life, we are called and chosen to reach the highest point –so we have the most perfectly freedom and the power to fight the lowermost things in ourselves with the power that God has given us for eternity.

If the Lord let man to care for his own physical needs so that the soul can practice self-cognition and act independently, how much more this is necessary for the soul itself? Even the souls of animals have an instinct of their own, according to which they act, each in its own way. It would be wrong to assume that these creatures, which are seemingly without speech and reason, perform their actions like machines, activated by an extrinsic force. If this were the case, even the best domestic animal could not be trained to perform the simplest task and would certainly not obey the call of man.

Since every animal has an individual soul possessing a separate vital force, by means of which the animal soul spontaneously activates its physical organism, an animal can be trained in different ways. A being that is animated merely from without has no memory nor is it capable of discernment. It lives mechanically and, where its aspirations are concerned, is limited and under judgment, so much so that any improvement through some kind of instruction is out of the question. That would also have to be done in a mechanical way from without.

You may tell a tree for a thousand years to stand in such and such a way and produce better fruit, but it will all be of no avail. You must put knife and saw into action, cut off wild branches, carefully split the stems and insert into them fresh branches of a better kind and then connect these well with the wild split stems. In this way, the mechanically grafted tree will then in the course of time produce better fruit.

Yet, you can train an animal even through words or through a special way of handling, and it will serve you as and when required and fully comply with your will. This gives you unmistakable proof that animals also have a kind of free will, without which they could no more obey and serve you than a stone or a tree.

If already animals evidently possess an individual soul endowed with some cognition and freedom of will that has to act independently, according to its own nature, to what higher degree, and how much more complex, this must be the case with a human soul?

Besides, the human soul is endowed with everything it needs for its progress in life. Once it has, through its own willpower and through the spontaneous love for God, moved into a mightier life-light, it will soon become aware of what it still lacks. It will then endeavor of its own free will to attain to this and, well recognizing the ways and means, strive for and grasp them, enriching herself with the treasures of the higher, more spiritual and more perfected life.

What the soul acquires on this road, which is a true road according to God's order, is and remains completely its own, and neither time nor eternity can tear it away from the soul. However, that which the soul could not itself have acquired through its volition and cognition, such as the external, physical body and with it some outer, worldly advantages, cannot remain with it but will be taken away just as it was given.

If that is how things are and what daily experience teaches man, there can be no question of evil, demonic influences affecting and determining the soul, for everything depends on the volition and cognition and, finally, the love of the soul. As you desire, understand and love, so it comes to you – it can never be possible otherwise!

If you desire, understand and love what is right according to God's order, you will in this way at all times attain to reality. However, if you desire, understand and love contrary to such order, which alone offers reality and substance, you are like a man who wants to harvest on a field where no grain was ever sown; and you have finally only to blame yourself if your life's harvest has come to nothing.

6.4 About freewill

God could coerce by His will all the people of the world to do good things; but that would also be a judgment which would turn a free man into a machine. If God will coerces us, then we are bound slaves, but if our own will move us, then we are free men; for our will now want what our mind, as the light of our soul, recognizes as true and good.

But it would be different with the world if it would be forced to act according to God's will; it would not recognize what is good and true and their actions would then be like that of an animal and even worse. For the animal stands on such a level that a force which is implanted in its nature cannot do any further moral damage to its soul, because the soul of an animal cannot have anything to do with a free moral code; but the soul of a free person would suffer great damage through an inner mechanical force, because the animal side would go quite against its free moral nature.

No one shall be coerced into anything. Whoever receives Christ, let him do so, and whoever wants to follow Him and His teaching, let him do likewise, because He and His kingdom are voluntary and therefore need to be gained in all freedom.

Only the freest self-determination counts with Him. Whatever is over or under that is without worth before Him and our Father. Every compulsion other than from the very own heart is foreign and cannot possibly be of any value for a person's very own life according to His eternal and, thus, freest order.

Of what use would it actually be to you if you claimed some work of art, which was created by another hand, to be your work? If then someone came and asked you to reproduce this work for a high reward, you would be ruined and before the whole world you will be called, a liar, cheat and boaster with another person's success, by the one who ordered the work.

Thus, the full cultivation of life has been put into every person's own hands. Before God's eyes, at every individual person's great life-trial, that which will be recognized as foreign to him, will be of no value and will be taken away. Then it will be said: "Who has, will keep what he has and will be given even much more, but who does not have his own, will forfeit what he has, since it is not his own, but only something foreign."

The men of the world are like wheat, barley and corn. This living grain however does not grow without chaff and the offensive dust. In order however for this grain (i.e. these worldly men) to be cleansed of their worldly chaff and filth and then, as a fully cleansed grain, to be gathered up into the Father's eternal barns, the followers of Christ are being transformed into proper and living winnowing fans, through whom the Father in Heaven shall cleanse His grain.

If a person trusts in God, he is trusted also by God, who does not forsake him and does not let him be confounded. But those who do believe in God's existence, but do not fully trust

Him, because their own heart tells them that they are unworthy of His help, are not helped by God either, for they have no trust in God. They trust only their own powers and means, which they regard as holy and inviolable as it were, and say: "Man, if you wish to be helped, help yourself, for charity begins at home and thus you have to look after yourself first." And by the time he has provided for himself, the one who needs help has perished!

If you provide for yourselves first, you are abandoned by God and are without His blessing and His otherwise so certain help. God did not create men for selfish reasons, but out of pure love and, therefore, men must in everything fully correspond to the love that gave them their existence.

If, however, you live and act without love and trust in God, you voluntarily reverse the heavenly element within you into a hellish one, turn away from God and become servants of Hell, which in the end will not fail to give you the reward you have deserved, which is death in the wrath of God.

Therefore go and care for your people, for your women and children, so that they would not go naked and not ever be plagued by hunger, or thirst. And it shall soon emerge how well you provided them therewith.

Whoever possesses property and has a trade which can give him a good profit, but saves the profit for himself and his children and looks with unkind eyes and heart down at the poor brothers and avoids the poor children who, because they lack all earthly goods, suffer hunger, thirst and cold and sends them away if they come to him asking for alms, and who says to a brother: "Come to me in a few days or weeks and then I will do this or that for you!" and when the hopeful, on help relying brother comes and reminds the one who promised of his promise, the latter excuses himself that also now he could not possibly help, while actually having the means to do it, in truth,

I tell you: that one is an enemy of God; how will he love God whom he does not see if he does not love his brother whom he sees before him and is aware of his misery?

In truth, in very truth I tell you: whoever forsakes his brother in need simultaneously forsakes God and Heaven also. And God will forsake him in the twinkling of an eye.

However, who does not forsake his poor brothers, not even if God sent him trials, shall be unexpectedly blessed temporally and eternally more richly than can anyone is here, on Earth.

On the other hand, it is good and right to punish sinners if they have strayed too much from the order which God Himself has set for certain perfection attainable in the shortest possible time. But no one should be prevented from the possibility of sinning through an inflexible "must"!

A sinner who voluntarily repents is more complete then 99 righteous living in accordance to the law, who never needed repentance. Of course, the one who is always a sinner become an animal which lives an unclean life prompted by a false instinctive motivation. A more complete man is the sinner who in himself freely recognizes that it was wrong to act contrary to the law and who begins to change his attitude according to the recognized order of God and becomes a man who is familiar with every lesson life teaches.

Once in the Kingdom of God, such a spirit will be capable of achieving endlessly greater things than one who out of slavish fear never strayed from the law by a hair's breadth and through this fear dictated observance of the law has physically and spiritually turned himself into a machine without a free will.

Take a stone and throw it upwards! In accordance with the "must" law put into it, it shall not take long for it to fall back to earth. Is the stone to be praised for keeping the law so strictly?

You can certainly do all sorts of things with the stone as far as a solid foundation is concerned; but create some free activity for it, and it shall not abandon its dead rest!

Hence one should not turn people into stones through "must" laws but rather educate them in their freedom, and then one have acted fully in accordance with God's order.

If the people highly placed upon earth were not as lazy as they are, with rare exception, they would with just a random amount of investigative spirit have quite easily noted that any person with a certain degree of education shall not in all eternity be satisfied with an animalistic monotony. He no longer builds a hut with thatches, straw and kneaded clay, but masons stones and bakes clay into bricks, building himself a stately dwelling with encircling walls, adding solid towers from whose battlements he can espy the approach of potential enemies.

And so a thousand educated people shall build themselves dwellings from which none resembles another – neither in shape nor interior design; in contrast, look at the nest of birds and animal retreats, and you shall never find diversification! Look at a swallow's or sparrow's nest or a spider's web or bee's cell and a thousand other products or efforts brought forth by animals, and you shall find neither an improvement, nor retrogression. But compare human works: what almost limitless diversity! And yet it is always only humans which bring all this about with often much effort!

This proves clearly that God, Who endowed man with a spirit similar to His own, did not create man to become an animal, but to gain the fullest and freest God-likeness. Just as the bird is incapable of flying without flying feathers, so also man's spirit cannot attain to a free life-activity, when his free cognition is trimmed by the sanctioned "must". A spirit without freewill is dead because he does not have what fundamentally conditions and comprises his life.

For his mere terrestrial life-sphere you can give man a thousand laws sanctioned under "must", and you will harm man's spirit therewith far less than if you sanction him even one divine Commandment terrestrially. The spiritual must remain free and has to determine the sanction freely within itself, as also the judgment associated therewith; only thus can it gain life's perfection in and out of itself. Free cognition of the good and true are the spirit's life-light; out of these he then himself determines laws that appeal to him. These are then free laws and the only ones harmonious to free life. The spirit's volition in accordance with his cognition is the free law within the spirit, and the necessity to eternally act in free will is the everlasting sanction in accordance with which no spirit surely shall act otherwise than in free volition.

God's freest will itself, in accordance with the most perfect cognition and wisest insights within Himself, determines the law, sanctioning it out of its very own, although admittedly free necessity. And this then is the basis of all created things, in so far as this is essential for the development, solidification and ultimate individualization of the Spirit.

The human spirit should become perfect in himself and by himself, like the primordial Spirit of God is in Himself and by Himself perfect; otherwise the Spirit is not spirit, but a judged death matter.

Every person has a completely free will according to which he can freely do what he wants, and therefore it is logical that his obedience depends on it. God Himself can and may never ever force him with His omnipotence, but He only can put man into such situations that by means of experiences he comes

– as if he achieved it himself – to a purer understanding and in this way He can guide his will by his own intellect.

But if God would, by His omnipotence and out of His wisdom, guide the will of man, then man would not be more than an animal. He even would be a little below it, for even to an animal a little freedom of will has been given – as experience can show you – and also an intellect and a memory. It can feel hunger, thirst and pain and therefore it is also able – although still vaguely – to think, and by its sound, facial expression and movements it can make known what it needs and wants.

O man, first of all recognize God and His almighty will properly, and you will then also recognize whether a man with a heart full of the Divine Spirit is really unable to will or do anything else but – in silent patience resigned to the eternal will of God – let one day after another pass while he happily watches the various herbs grow and flower and again wither away!

If that would have been God's aim with the people, He never would have needed to give them their own free will, all He had to do was to simply let them grow like the mushrooms of the Earth with the roots stuck in the soil, just like sea polyps, but in human form; these would then have been able to look on day and night to see how the stars rise and set according to the will of God, at least the way it seems, and how beautifully the grass grows around them! A free movement would not be necessary at all for them for they would in any case not have a free will, and the unchanging and stereotypical will of God could let them go much better as statues rather than as any pious person devoted to God with his will!

For despite all his aesthetics, it can still come into the sense of a person, who still has his own will and a free movement, to take a few steps across a beautiful grassy ground. Inevitably, he presses the grass that has grown upright according to the will and the eternal order of God; and beside this trespassing, he kills the life of a few grass mites before their time!

Or now consider that a person for his physical nutrition does not only chew up with his teeth all sorts of magnificent fruits filled to brimming with fruit seeds and then consumes them as meals for his body without any mercy or compassion, but instead even attacks all sorts of animals, kills them and finally consumes their roasted flesh with a true selfishness. Here and there he seeks special places where previously for many millennia the most beautiful plants, healing herbs, bushes and trees have grown in the most beautiful and very most undisturbed order of God, and then builds dead houses and cities on this spot.

Or, if you shorten your nails, beard and hair that have grown too long with time, are you not acting against the order of God, according to whose stereotypical will, your nails, beard and hair grow again immediately and do not want to remain as short as you have decided yourselves with the scissors?

If God did not want at all some free-thinking and free-desiring being to act against the stereotype of His creating will and to make destructive attacks against the existing constantly unchangingly same order in big things as well as in small, would He have acted wisely to create beings that for the very sake of their existence are forced to make all sorts of destructive intrusions into the original order of creation, which is also a work of the same all-powerful and highly wise God?!

And if God, the Lord and Creator of all things and beings, allows the living beings, and namely the free-thinking people who are equipped with a free will, to destroy the forests, cut down the trees, build huts and houses out of it while burning the greatest part, trample His beautiful grass into the ground, mow it and feed it as hay to the cows, oxen, donkeys, sheep and goats and does not repent for many other transgressions of His set order, then how much less will He use His almightiness to put up opposition when it means developing man's little freedom of will into the greatest divine one?

If one keep the easy commandments of God and truly love God above all, one will become obviously more united with the recognition and desires of God. One will become wiser and wiser and to the same degree also more powerful and insightful in desires.

Your inner light from God will be raised to an all-seeing eye, with the means of which you will not feel anymore the otherwise still dark life, but instead you will see the effective powers of life and through the possession of the freest will of God be able to decide as well to be active in one way or another. But only in this way, that you recognize and see specially and individually the countless powers constantly coming from God, you can, as a possessor of the divine will, seize them and also determine them and bind them to some wise goal, and they will immediately be just as active as if God had determined them for some action Himself.

For all the powers that proceed from God through all the whole infinity are just like the countless arms of one and the same all-powerful God and can impossibly become and be active in any other way, other than through the stimulus of the divine will, because they are basically nothing but pure emissions of the divine will.

6.5 *About disciples*

The birds have their nests and the foxes their dens; but Christ has nowhere to lay His head! Whoever wants to follow

Him, or become His disciple, must take a heavy burden onto his back and follow Him like that! Earthly advantages for His disciples there are none; on the contrary, in His name and for the sake of His love they have to leave their earthly advantages, not only for a time, but for ever; even wives and children must not hinder them, if they want to become true disciples of the Kingdom of God.

They are not allowed to have money or other worldly treasures, not even two tunics, no shoes unless necessary, only sacks to fill or a stick or hiking staff to defend themselves against a possible enemy.

They are not allowed to have anything on Earth, but alone the hidden secret of the Kingdom of God. If you can bring yourself to accept this, then you can be His disciple!

Every one of His disciples must also be full of love, gentleness and patience towards every man, just as He is. He must bless his worst enemy just as much as his best friend and must, when the opportunity arises, do good even to the one who has done him harm beforehand, and pray for those who persecute him.

Anger and revenge must be far from the heart of anyone who wants to be His disciple; he must not complain about the bitter events on this Earth or even begin to grumble about it in annoyance.

He must flee all the pleasures of sensual life, but summon up everything to create a new spirit in his heart through God living word and finally, for eternity, live on completely in this spirit in the fullness of all spiritual power.

Whoever loves Jesus Christ and actively believes that he is the One whose descent the fathers awaited, he is also fully with Christ, as He is fully one with Our Father in Heaven! For love joins everything; God and Creation become one through it, and no space can ever separate what the true and pure love from the deepest depths of Heaven has joined.

The heart of a person who is closely connected to God has alone the goal of seeking God and also finding Him and then taking a new, indestructible life from out of this God once found. But whoever seeks God with his other senses can find Him just as little as a man who binds his eyes can find and see the sun with his ears, or nose.

The correct and living sense of the heart is love. Whoever awakens the innermost sense of life and begins to seek God with it, must certainly find Him, just as well as a person who, if he is not fully blind, must find the sun with his eye and see its light.

And whoever wants to hear a wise word must not cover his ears and try to hear it with the eyes; for the eyes certainly see the light and all the illuminated forms, but the more spiritual form of the word cannot be seen, instead only heard with the ear.

6.6 *The Gordian knot*

Whatever you can see and feel by means of the flesh has affinity with the flesh and its tools, and is similarly changeable and transitory; so, whatever is changeable and transitory, how could the same offer you substance for ever-constant and immortal truth?

There is only one thing in man, and this great and holy One is love, which is a proper fire out of God, dwelling in the heart; within this is true, and nowhere else, because love is itself the arch-foundation of all truth in God, and out of God within every man.

If you want to see and recognize things in yourself in their full truth, then you have to see and recognize them from this solely true arch-foundation of your being; everything else is delusion, and man's head and what is in it belongs to the sphere of your familiar Gordian knot, which no one can untie with mere deliberation.

Only with the cutting power of the spirit of love in man's own heart can he hew through this knot, and then begin to think, see and recognize in the heart, and only then along such path to get at the truth of his own and every other being and life.

Your head can create countless gods for you, but what are they? Nothing but vain, lifeless patterns produced by the brain with its loose mechanisms. Only in the heart shall you find a God, and this One is true, because the love in which you found the only true God is itself Truth.

This Truth therefore can be sought and found only in Truth, but the head has done its share if it has delivered you the key to Truth. Yet everything that urges and draws you towards love can be a key to truth; therefore, follow such attraction and urge and enter upon the love of your heart, and you shall find the truth which shall free you from all deception.

Abide in pure love and act within its truth and power, and you shall be finding truth everywhere, and quite evidently perceive that there is universal truth indeed which penetrates not only this Earth, but all of infinity.

If you were to act towards mankind in that way then you would quite legitimately follow Christ, and through such imitation win eternal life. Because verily, this earth-life lasts for a time, and then comes eternity.

6.7 *Science and faith*

All around us, what you see with your eyes, hear with your ears and perceive with your senses, are all embodied thoughts of God. You see the mighty movement of the waves. The whole sea, all the mountains, all the animals, all grass, herbs and trees, all the people, the sun, the moon and all the countless many stars are nothing else but embodied thoughts of God. There being solely depends on the incomprehensible permanence of the will of God.

If God would withdraw His will from one of these embodied thoughts, that embodiment would cease to exist in the same moment. The spiritual thought in God still exists, but the body would so to speak dissolve into pure nothingness.

Even the little clouds in the sky, how they get bigger and then become small again and soon disappear altogether, these are also thoughts of God, which are obviously closer to the original spiritual elements, than the solid mountains and all the other forms, which surround us to all sides; but their existence is nevertheless imperfect and by a repeated appearance they first must change into another form, like for example a drop of rain, and then as nutrient in one or other plant take on a more concrete and durable shape, and this continues up to humans, where they become totally free and independent and self freely thinking and free willing beings, forever unchangeable and durable, and where they can and also will go over to the pure spiritual and God resemblance. Who looks at the creatures of God in this manner, finds a lot of joy and happiness in it!

Some of Jesus followers took him for a very wise and highly accomplished doctor and when they saw him accomplish unusual deeds, they began to take him for a prophet through whom God's Spirit acted. But being among them several experienced men, they felt prompted to find out how he had achieved such perfection. Thereupon, Jesus revealed to them what he is and what is in him, and also what can become of man when he has fully recognized himself, achieving by that the fullest life-liberty of his spirit.

This was a purposeful preparation of their souls and spirits, so that they could watch Him performing divine miracles, without being harmed. Because they accepted freely and that in a fully scientific way, that God can be a man and man can be a god.

But it is quite different with other people, which are not open to the scientific approach. These only have faith and otherwise little understanding.

The faith of the soul however is nearer to life than the most perfect intellect. However, if the faith is a coerced one, then it also becomes a shackle to the soul. If the soul is shackled, then there can be no talk of the development of the spirit within it.

But where the intellect first was brought to the right insight, there the soul remains free and takes for herself light from the intellect to the extent of her tolerance and digestive capacity.

And thus through a properly educated intellect, a true, full and living faith develops, from which the spirit within the soul receives the right nutrients, becoming steadily stronger and mightier, which can be perceived by any man whose love towards God and neighbor gets steadily stronger and mightier.

But as stated, where man's intellect quite often is undeveloped, man having only faith, which in its confined state is as it were only an obedience to the heart and its will, such person must then be approached with caution, for it not to go numb with delusion, or be hideously side-tracked, as it is only too obviously and unfortunately the case with all heathens and others at this time. Therefore, no blind should lead another, otherwise they both will fall into the abyss.

I say unto you all, to be assiduous and acquire a proper knowledge in all things. Examine everything you encounter and retain only what is good and true and you shall find it easy to grasp the truth and enliven the formerly dead faith, making it into a true lantern of life.

If you want to reap the proper benefit from Christian teaching, then you must first understand it and only then truly act in accordance with the truth. Just as the Father in Heaven is perfect in all things, even so you too must be perfect; otherwise, you cannot become His children.

6.8 About the will power

The will of a person is twofold: one will is where the recognition of the truth lays, and always has a somewhat weak hauling or guiding rope; the other will is where the sensuous world with its joyous smelling demands also has a hauling rope, which by all kinds of habits has become quite strong and powerful. If the world shows you a pleasant bite together with the possibility to obtain it, then the strong rope starts to strongly pull at the will cluster of the heart; even if at the same time the lesser strong haul-and-guide rope of the truth recognition begins to stir, it is of little or no use, because the strong has always carried victory over the weak.

The will that should be effective, must act with serious determination and not be afraid of anything. With the most stoic detachment it must be able to laugh off all the advantages of the world and even at the cost of its bodily life it must follow the bright path of truth. Only then the usually the weak recognition of the truth will become strong and mighty and the purely worldly emotion and pleasure will completely become subservient. Finally, the latter will also completely transform itself into the light of true cognition, and so man will finally become united in himself, which is of the greatest essential importance for the inner perfection of the immortal human being.

Because in your thoughts you cannot agree with yourself, how can you then say: "I have recognized the truth in its depth and fullness!" In yourself you are still in complete disagreement and therefore in yourself you are nothing then a pure lie. The lie is in contrast to the truth like the thickest night in comparison to the brightest day. In such a night there is no light, and man in himself a lie, cannot recognize the bright truth. Therefore in all worldly people, who are still full of disagreement, the haul and guide rope of recognition of the truth will become so weak, that at the slightest pull of the worldly pleasure it will be broken and thereby defeated.

When, in some people, the worldly pleasure will has defeated and crushed the will for the recognition of the truth, a kind of unity of darkness occurs in the inner man, which has become dead in the Spirit and is thereby condemned in himself and cannot get to the light anymore, except through the fire of his coarse matter, ignited by the pressure of worldly desires. Fortunately, the matter of the soul is many times more resilient as this of the body and a quite powerful fire is required in order to consume and destroy all the soul-matter.

Since such a soul will not allow the exceedingly painful and necessary purification to happen to her, for the sake of love for the truth or the light, but instead will try to avoid it (out of its old pleasure and gloomy lust for power), that person, who in this world has become completely united in his night of life, is therefore almost lost forever.

Only the person who, by his energetic clear recognition will, has completely defeated the worldly pleasure will, in himself has become unified in the light and in all truth and as such also in life itself. But for that, it requires a truly stoic self-denial, but of course not that of your haughty Diogenes, who thought he was more and higher than gold shining king Alexander, but a humble self-denial like Enoch, Abraham, Isaac and Jacob. If you can do this, you will be helped for life and forever; but if you can`t do that, and not out of your own strength of truth recognition, then it is over with you, and you cannot be helped on this side, nor the other.

6.9 To be born again

That, which is born out of the flesh, is flesh, and that which is born out of the spirit, is spirit. Do not be surprised about what I said to you: you must be born again!

The wind blows to where it wants, and although you can hear its rustle, you do not know from where it originated and where it goes. So is everyone who is born out of the spirit. Although you can see and hear him, but because he speaks to you in his spiritual way, you do not understand or perceive what he says or from where it comes what he says, neither what he means by that. This can happen, because what we know and understand, we know and understand through our bodies. When our bodies will be taken away from us, we will hardly understand and perceive anything terrestrial. Then, how can we turn from body into spirit and how can a spirit then have another spirit and give birth again?

The spirit which is spirit in itself, can only know what spirit is and what its life is about. The fleshes however is only an outer bark and know nothing of the sprit, unless the spirit reveals it to the covering, the bark. Even more, when a spirit is still too much controlled and covered by flesh it does not know it, only when your spirit will become free, he will know.

In truth, in very truth I tell you: "Unless a man has been born over again, he cannot see the Kingdom of God, least of all enter it". Which is to say: "If you do not awaken your spirit (through ways shown you by the Word) and act, you cannot even recognize the divine life within God, let alone penetrate into its life-giving depths!"

The soul must be cleansed first with the water of humility and self-denial (for water is the most ancient symbol of humility, it allows everything to be done with it, serves in all things and always seeks for itself the lowest places on Earth, fleeing the heights) and only after by the spirit of truth, which an impure soul cannot ever conceive. An impure soul is like the night, whereas truth is a sun full of light, which causes to be day all around it.

Since the true blissfulness of life does not consist of clear visioning and understanding, but only of the activity of love that should increase more and more, every soul should first make this his only life's purpose, for he otherwise can never attain to the inner clearness of life, because the activity of love is an inner fire of life, which must become a bright light-giving flame by its increasing activity.

However, when this life's purpose in the soul is completely awakened, in such a way that the soul himself becomes this life principle element – which means to say that the whole man is born anew and thus born again in the spirit – then the soul stays also active in the highest possible degree, despite his inner clearness which is a result of the activity of love raised to the highest possible level. And his blissfulness and clearness will increase according to the degree of his activity of love and not according to the degree of his knowledge, to which at no time he can attain without the activity of love, because God has determined since eternity that no spirit and no human soul can ever attain to the divine light without the corresponding activity.

How do people in this material world make light? Look, they rub wood against wood or stone against stone, just as long as fire sparks will come off. The fire sparks fall on lightly inflammable material that maintain the glow. Once that glow is sufficiently present, and inflammable objects come in contact with it – like wood, straw or a certain lightly inflammable resin mixed with sulfur and naphtha – then soon a bright flame will flare up and it will become light in himself and around him into all directions.

Look, in this way, already the dead material world shows that in order to make fire and light a certain activity must precede. Thus, to the light of the soul's life must all the more precede a certain activity. By this, love will be awakened, which is the life element, and only from then on, the light of the soul will exist from its increased activity, and this is the wisdom, which recognizes, evaluates and orders itself and all things out of itself.

This is how things are concerning the life of the soul and her inner clear ability to recognize herself, and so you should not be afraid that a blessed soul will ever become lazy and passive as a result of her divine wisdom, because the wisdom of a soul here, and still more in the beyond, will always be the result of her activity. If this activity would or could cease, then the soul and his wisdom and his inner clearness of life would cease to exist.

Therefore, whoever absorbs truth into his soul cleansed through humility and really recognizes this as such is set free in spirit through this truth. This freedom of the Spirit, or the entering of the Spirit into such freedom, is then also the actual spiritual birth, which is the only gate to the Kingdom of God.

6.10 The missing link

Man lives in two kinds of worlds, which he has to unite in himself. On the one hand he is the cornerstone of the outer, material creation, in which he is called the crown of creation and he is praised as such. On the other hand, he is the starting point of the pure spiritual world, which with him has reached the first stage of complete free self-awareness. So, on the one hand he is the beginning of chain and, on the other hand, the end of a chain, and he has to find in himself (for that purpose life was given and its free development) the missing link with which he can make those two chains as one.

All beings, from the smallest creature, form a step to step ascending series, in such manner that one step will always complete the other, will show greater perfections and can by that also develop an ever greater intelligence.

Look at the small animals, which seem to have no other goal than to maintain their body and serve as food for other animals. When there is a predator of their body and life, they stoically surrender to their fate and do not fight back and are also not capable to do that. However, further up you can see that the intelligence is already developed and those big animals are more conscious of the dangers that threaten their bodies, and also know how to escape from them through all kinds of cunning tricks.

With animals that are more advanced you can see that this quality is further developed, and so they are provided with suitable weapons like sharp claws and teeth to get rid of their enemies, but at the same time they become also enemies of other animals. Now there is a struggle from both sides where cunningness and cleverness are practiced, to kill the bodies but also for the progression of the intellect so that the character, that gradually develops and that acquires specific qualities for the ever ascending animals, can be formed.

A borderline is reached from which the animals are inclined to join man, and then you call them house animals. They usually are more submissive or tamer as you say. They can develop a very far-reaching intelligence and can be trained. By that they look in a certain way more like humans – not in their outer form but for what concerns certain characteristics. You often can observe real astonishing actions of animals that show reasoning and also a certain discernment so that you are amazed and say: the animal lacks only the power of speech. Look, these are animals that in their spiritual development only need to make one step further to become a human being, like an infant who has also only to make a certain step in years in order to become a person with reason. But with the animal that goal cannot be attained, because the form of the soul is not perfected yet, while with a child, who often seems much dumber and clumsier, the form of the soul is present and capable for a further development, like in every grain of seed in which lays the image of the future plant.

All these sorts of animals, which are multiple in order to make possible an optimal variety in character abilities, are however under a fixed law, which takes care that they can evolve in that one certain direction, namely the one of the highest possible intelligence. This means they are not capable to act differently than the limits of the form of their soul will permit. For instance, no matter how clearly you will indicate to a bird that it still would be better not to build an open nest but perhaps a woven house, it will nevertheless stay with his nest.

And you can be sure that since the existence of the different sorts on Earth every sort built their homes exactly as they still do today.

This is in a certain way because of a limited horizon (the form of the soul) that cannot be extended. It is just like a child who cannot learn the difficult higher arithmetic as long as he still does not understand the initial basics.

The different forms that the animals must go through correspond to the time periods or years of development of man. When the highest animal intelligence is developed – mind you, this is not concerning the outer form, but only concerning the development of the soul – then those developed intelligences can flow together to become a human soul. So, this contains now in the first place the highest developed intelligences that mutually complement each other, and then, since he is the next step in the development of many lower lives, he must be a reflection of the total lower life in general, because he contains all this in himself. So the human soul is now completed for what concerns the outer form and the inner form that is capable for development. The crown of creation, the human form, with a germ that is capable for the highest possible development, is reached in the newly born human being.

Now begins the second task: man must reach the highest possible free awareness in the knowledge of his Creator and in the development of the inner man.

Up to now the form of the soul was dull, did not care about spiritual things, but only about material things. Only the right of the strongest was important to him. But the deity wants the fulfillment of His work, which was led here with difficulty, so the creature will have to begin to know Him and will try to come closer to Him out of love, and not out of fear for His power. How can this be achieved?

The Deity must veil Himself to reach that goal. That means that He must put His creature in circumstances that gives him the possibility to recognize the deity freely from himself, or not. By that, the Deity may not use any coercion, for otherwise fear, which has to be avoided, and not love will influence the direction of the will. Just think how you would feel to be surrounded by servants who would only serve you out of fear, instead of out of love!

That little plant of love can only come into existence when the human soul receives proof – by the ever increasing clearness and insight of things – of the great love and wisdom which the Deity gives him and which stirs up admiration and love in him.

A leader is now given to the human soul, because the pure soul alone, which cannot be further developed as perfected form, would not notice anything higher than him if a spiritual feeling could not flow in, the awareness of a power in him, which humbles him down and urges him to seek his Creator. And this is the divine spark which is laid in him as spirit and which has to develop together with him, has to penetrate in him more and more through a right education and must lead him into all knowledge through self-teaching.

This true marriage, which starts already when man is born, is however greatly disturbed because, although the soul is developed by the inevitable physical development, the inner spirit stays mostly only like an embryo in him. However, the purpose of life is to let them develop together at the same time so that the one depends in the right measure on the other.

The Spirit, that divine spark, comes from God and contains initially all the truth and the right knowledge. By that spark, man stands in very close connection with the initial Spirit of God Himself and he can penetrate in all secrets and the wisdom of God Himself. But very few people are aware of this!

But this will happen only when man has found the binding link of the chain, which is the divine teaching which comes from God, and has connected both chains in one unbreakable chain. If not, one is completely powerless as the last link of the material chain and is actually nothing but a very intelligent, well developed animal.

Despite the great many various notions and ideas that a soul can develop out of himself with only little training, and which he also can imagine – correctly or less correctly, that is for the moment the same – if he would not be as a whole, like a unity that contains everything in itself, he would be capable as less as an ox or a donkey to design the construction of a royal castle and build it according to that design.

If you consider all the various animals in the air, like the insects and birds, as well as the animals on the solid surface of the Earth, and those in the water, then you will discover with most of them the capability to build something. Just look at the bees and other little animals in the air that more or less look like it. Look at the very various nests of the birds, and the ants and still other insects in the soil, the spiders and the caterpillars. Furthermore, look at all sorts of mouse, the beaver that builds a precise hut, the foxes, wolves, bears and still a great number of other animals, and see how they build and arrange their habitations very efficiently for themselves. Look at the various animals in the sea, especially the crustaceans. Then you will see with them such great capability to build that it often even very much amazes the best architect.

Now, every animal, from the smallest to the biggest, has of course its own very simple building capability that is typical to the intelligence of its animal soul. It moreover knows the building material and always uses it in its own way and manner. But in the human soul a very large number of all those animal-intelligent building capabilities are present, and from them, the man can, as it were through a silent awareness, put also a very large number of concepts and ideas together, and so he can create completely new and great forms.

And so man can invent, when he is somehow developed, all kinds of houses in a very large variety, and countless other things, and also accomplish them with his will, reason and zeal. Could he do that if in his soul all those various capabilities would not be present in the manner that was described above? Certainly not, for even the next most intelligent animal after man has no imagination and has therefore also no all-embracing talent to give form to things.

In the two commandments: "Love God above all and your fellowman like yourself" are contained all the 10 commandments of Moses and all the rest about what man should do to awaken the spiritual spark that abides in him and to unite more and more with his soul. For it is only in the right way of living according to God and in the right deeds of love for your fellowman that you will find true satisfaction, inner peace and the right victory over your passions and death. The one in whom the faith is awakened, which makes it impossible for him to sin against those commandments, will already discover true Heaven on this Earth, for he became untouchable for all the attacks of evil, became by that a real ruler in him, and out of him a ruler over nature.

Since the soul of man contains everything from all the beings that the Earth carries, it is very natural that once the Spirit will rule in his house, he will be able to rule over everything around him. Just like a king, who worked himself up from the rank of slave to the throne, will rule without resistance over all these ranks to which he belonged.

7 The Practice

7.1 *About virtue and vice*

One might well say here and there and also judge: Yes, yes, it is good to preach about the virtue of generosity and to present greed as a most despicable vice; but who could actually help the fact that the overwhelming tendency towards wasteful generosity has a strong motive in one person, while for another it is the very sheerest greed?! For both people it is the same thing, an external appearance of their inner love, from which a blessed feeling awakes of its own accord which he then, like every other, keeps for himself. But the first man only becomes sad if he does not possess such abundance that he cannot make his poor neighbors happy, and the second becomes sad when he does not receive as much as he wishes – or even loses! That being so, everything lays in the nature of the person from his origin, and then basically there can be neither a vice nor a true virtue. For the greedy person generosity is a vice – and for the generosity greed is just as much so. Can water help the fact that it must be of a softer and more flexible nature, and who can damn a stone because of its hardness?! The water must be what it is, and likewise the stone.

On the one hand, this is certainly true; it is the nature of the generous to be generous and the nature of avarice is the exact opposite. But the matter stands thus: Every human is born as a child with the impulse for selfishness and avarice, and such a soul always has within it the coarsest material animal element, which applies particularly to those souls that are not from above, but only from this earth. However, also the souls coming from the stars to this earth are not quite free of this element.

If man is brought up in this animalistic element, he transforms it more and more into his own life's ground, i.e. into his love. But because this is so animal-like, man remains a wild animal and has nothing human about him but the miserable form, the loosened tongue and due to the orderly construction of his brain a good capacity for cognition which, however, is more and more activated into base activity by the animal element. It can, therefore, recognize as good and conducive to bliss only that which the purely animalistic elements wants.

Therefore, if someone wishes to maintain that, in the real meaning of truth there is no virtue and, thus, no vice – and one who thinks that it is wrong to condemn avarice as opposed to generosity, let him be referred to this explanation; let him consider and ponder it well.

But if a gardener plants two fruit trees in his garden and cares for them as he should, it will be of no matter to him if only one of the trees bears fruit, but the other (being of the same kind and standing in the same earth, nourished by the same rain and dew, the same air and the same light) does not bear any fruit, nor even a satisfactory canopy, to provide shade? I think the insightful gardener will say then: "that is an undutiful, ill tree which consumes all the juices that come to it; we have to see whether it cannot be helped, or not!" Then the gardener will try all the means he knows and if all these means do not help, in the end he will cut down the unfruitful, ruined tree and plant another one in its place.

A miserly and selfish man is a spoilt man, within and through himself, and cannot bear any fruit of life, because he consumes all life within him. On the other hand, a generous person is already in the correct order of life, because he bears abundant fruit outwardly. But a tree cannot help the fact that it bears fruit or not; for it does not form the fruit itself, but the spirits rising in its organism from the just richness of nature form them through its power and through the highly simple and therefore also very limited intelligence. But man stands on a point through which the unlimited intelligence of his soul begins to form and to transform itself into a tree bearing the richest abundance of fruit of life.

If he does that, for which he has all the means, only then will he become a true person in the true, eternal order of God; but if he does not do that, he remains an animal which has no free life in itself as such and therefore also cannot bring any life to his neighbor through good and kind deeds.

It is already explained that God on this Earth did not want nor could have created the Earth itself and everything that it contains for an eternal existence. On this Earth, everything is changeable and perishable, and it is only a point of transition from the first judgment and death to the true, eternal unchangeable life.

The deity with His almightiness can make it happen that man, just like the plants and the animals, must live in a certain order, but then man would not be man anymore, for then he will have no insight, no reason and also no free will of himself. But since the deity did not want that, based on highly wise grounds, He gave man insight, reason and a free will, and with that also the ability to become similar to God by developing and completing himself spiritually.

That humanity is neglected by the current education, while the deity excellently provided for that education since the very first beginning, and that is only because of the vice of laziness of the people. If nowadays there are still honorable and just men among the people, then why are they not all honorable and just?

Just because they are lazy!

That is why the deity, from time to time, let the civilizations to be destroyed, because laziness and the resulting immorality were dominating there. If the civilizations would have remained honorable and just, the deity would not have send enemies against them, but would have preserved them. The reason why they were destroyed is that their plague of laziness would finally have spoiled and ruined the whole population of the Earth.

At no time did the deity let these nations be without wise teachers, and many better people who lived in those cities were still saved by them, but those who were too lazy had finally to be removed together with their habitations.

A wise government for whom a good order is important by means of its laws will surely also call a willful transgressor to account and chastise him. Should then the deity, no matter how good and indulgent He is, also not chastise a too degenerated people and wake them up with a just rod out of the big laziness and lead them to activity?

You will realize that this is necessary. On a globe where man cannot sink into all the greatest vices by his free will, his intellect and his reason, he can also not raise himself to the highest and divine virtue. To create and raise animals, trees and plants is easy for the deity, but to educate people is not so easy. The deity can only educate them, but cannot enforce an internal coercion on them.

7.2 *About being active*

When someone has walked a long distance and finally reaches a shelter, if he does not go to bed immediately, but continues with small activities, on the following day will be on his feet already before sunrise, not feeling any tiredness. The longer he will thus continue his journey, the less tired it will make him.

However, if someone, after a day's march arrives quite tired at a shelter and immediately throws himself on a bed and maybe leaves it only at noon on the following day, he will be continuing his journey on completely stiff feet and with a totally drunk head. After having covered a certain distance, from utter exhaustion long rest he will collapse on the road and perishes there, if no one comes to his aid.

What has caused it? His own too great desire for rest and the delusion that rest strengthens a person.

If someone wish to achieve a great, amazing accomplishment in one or the other art, where a high degree of skillfulness of hands and fingers is required, then I ask you: will he achieve it if instead of constant diligent practice every day he idly strolls around day by day with his hands in his pockets motivated by a kind of anxious concern not to tire his hands and fingers to prevent them from getting stiff and unfit for the striven-for accomplishment?

Truly, even Christos with his boundless wisdom could not be a prophet and determine the time when such a disciple of art will become a virtuoso.

Only activity upon activity for the common good of people brings our salvation. For all life is the fruit of God's constant, never tiring activity and therefore can only be maintained and preserved for eternity through proper activity, whereas nothing but death does and must result from inactivity.

Place your hands on your heart and feel how it is constantly active, day and night. The life of the body depends solely on such activity. Once the heart stops, that would mean the end of the natural life of the body. Just as the rest of the physical heart obviously constitutes the total death of the body, this same rest of the soul's heart is the death of the soul.

However, the heart of the soul is called love, and its pulsating expresses itself in true and full love-activity. Thus constant love-activity is the never wearying pulse-beat of the soul's heart. The more actively the heart of the soul pulsates, the more life is generated in the soul and once there is a sufficiently high degree of life, this awakens therein the life of the divine Spirit.

This Spirit – being pure life because it is the untiring supreme activity itself – then flows into the soul that has become equal to it through love activity, and everlasting imperishable life has fully begun within the soul. And all this arises from activity, but never from idle rest. Therefore, shun rest and seek full activity, and eternal life will be your reward.

Do not imagine that Jesus have come to bring peace to mankind on this Earth. O no, only the sword and war instead. For, men must be impelled to all kinds of activity through distress and hardships or they would become lazy, fatted oxen that fatten themselves for eternal death. Distress and hardship bring about fermentation upon fermentation in man from which in the end something spiritual could develop.

One could, of course, say: "Through distress and hardship also anger, vengeance, murder and manslaughter arise, also envy, hardheartedness and persecution." That is indeed true, but bad as all that is, the result is nevertheless better than from idle rest which is dead and brings neither good nor bad results.

Moreover, spiritual works and spiritual ways are not meted in hours and meters, but entirely according to the power of the will, the faith and the love for God and fellowman.

He who could at once deny himself in such a way that he gives up everything that is of the world and – in the right measure – would give his treasures to the poor, only out of pure love for God, and would not yield to the flesh of women, would truly be perfected in a very short time. But he, who obviously needs more time to purify himself of the earthly dross and appendages, must also wait longer until he reaches the complete happy making state of true spiritual perfection.

A highly ranked statesman must exercise his profession, and no obstacle could keep him away from walking rightly. But he has to avoid thinking that he is the office and the honor and the respect of the office. Honor and respect of the office is the law, and he is only its laborer.

If we are faithful, good and honest in our actions, then we are partakers of the honor and the respect of the others and we are peaceful and safe, and this will then also be to our advantage before the face of God.

An extremely rich men, for whom his riches are no obstacles for the attainment of the pure spiritual state, he will handle it well, being not thrifty and stingy by the support of the poor, with true love for God and for fellowman, like good and wise fathers towards their children.

In the same measure in which we are showing love to the poor, God will always reward us spiritually and if necessary also naturally.

If you think that God is not helping at all the one who, with full dedication continuous to walk seriously on the way to God's Kingdom and to the life of the spirit, when now and then he becomes tired and weak, then you are greatly mistaken. Once he who has in all seriousness set foot on that way, will also without knowing it be helped by God in order to progress and finally also to certainly reach the goal.

Of course, God will not compel with His omnipotence the unification of the soul with the Spirit out of Him, but He will enlighten the heart of man more and more and fill it with true wisdom from the Heavens, and by that, man will grow spiritually and become stronger and will be able to conquer easier and with more confidence all obstacles, which for his greater trial could still come on his path.

The more love for God and his fellowman one will truly begin to feel and the more merciful one becomes in his mind, the greater and stronger has then also become the Spirit out of God in one's soul, because the love for God and from that to fellowman is now exactly God's Spirit in the soul of man. To the same extend as this love will increase and grow, also God's Spirit will grow in him. And when finally the whole man has become pure and charitable love, then the complete unification of the soul with God's Spirit in him has taken place. Then man has reached forever the supreme goal in life that God had set for him.

If the soul will, by his free will, become completely like the love of the Spirit out of God, then it is also clear that he will become one with the Spirit out of God that is in him. And when he will become like that, then he is also perfected. And of this, no certain time can be determined. However, the soul's own feeling must say and indicate this.

True, pure and living love is in itself completely unselfish. It is full of humility, active, full of patience and compassion. It will never unnecessary burden anyone and will gladly tolerate everything. It does not take pleasure in the need of its fellowman, but is always trying to help everyone who needs help.

Pure love is chaste in the highest degree and has no joy in the lustfulness of the flesh. But the purity of the heart is all the more pleasing to him.

If the soul of man will also become like that by his actions of his free will, then the soul is as his spirit and is then also perfected in God.

7.3 *Nothing but the truth*

Do not ever promise a person something you then cannot or – even worse – do not wish to keep for whatever reasons, if you truly want to become children of God. In truth, I tell you, the worst thing is a promise that is not kept. The one who is angry sins within himself and harms first himself. Who practices lewdness buries his soul in the judgment of the flesh and again harms himself. But the evil of all evils is the lie.

If you have promised to do something for a person and circumstances arise that make it impossible for you to keep your promise, do go to him without delay and tell him honestly what has happened to you, so that he can help himself at the proper time in some other way to overcome some difficulty.

But woe betides everyone who makes promises and does not keep them, for thereby he causes far-reaching trouble. The one who expected his help cannot fulfill his duty, and the hands of those who relied on him are tied, and thus such a broken promise can cause greatest embarrassment and distress to thousands. Therefore, a promise that is not kept is the thing most opposed to the love of one's neighbor and, therefore, the greatest of evils.

It is better to have a hard heart, because that will not raise any deceptive hopes with anyone. One knows that no help can be expected from a hard-hearted person and, therefore, other means are sought for the preservation of the necessary order. But if someone expects something that was promised to him, he abstains from seeking other ways and means, and when the time comes that the business of the one expecting help has to be attended to and the one who promised him lets him down and does not tell him in advance that for some reason, which must of course be absolutely true, he will not be able to keep his promise, such promiser is like Satan who from the very beginning made mankind brilliant promises through his followers, and none of which he has ever kept, thereby plunging numerous people into misery.

Therefore, beware above all of such promises which you cannot keep and, even worse, for whatever reasons do not want to keep, for that is the attitude of the chief of devils.

7.4 About service

To serve is the great password through all the spheres of infinity, in the great kingdom of nature, as well as the endless kingdom of the spirits!

Also, the inhabitants of hell understand this – only with the immense difference between "serving" of the inhabitants of the heavens; in hell basically everybody wants to be served; and if someone serves another, this is only eye-service, thus always a highly self-interested pretended service, whereby the one wants to deceive the other, to make sure to get him even better under his claws at another opportunity, and to draw an advantage for himself from his downfall.

For that reason, a hellish soul lifts his superiors upwards, like a certain kind of vulture along the shore of the sea does this with tortoises. Such a serviceable vulture sees a tortoise creeping around a marsh. The toad tries to reach land to search for herbs to satisfy its hunger. The flesh-hungry vulture first provides it with the service to lift it out of the marsh and puts it on dry land full of herbs. Soon the toad starts to search for the nourishing herbs. The vulture watches it for a while and makes only subtle attempts to test the hardness of its shell. Since its sharp beak cannot shear a piece of meat from the shell, it leaves the poor toad grazing quietly until it sticks its head out of the shell more courageously and perky, avaricious for the herbs.

When the vulture notices such confidence of the toad, it grabs the soft, fleshy head with its claws and lifts the toad high into the air and carries it to a place where it notices a hard rocky surface. There it let's go of the lifted toad, and its deadly downfall begins. Reaching the rocky ground quickly as an arrow, it smashes into pieces, and the vulture who accompanied its victim with the same speed, is equally quickly at hand to take the reward for its earlier diligent service and to stuff its continuously hungry stomach. There you have a true picture of nature for the hellish service diligence.

This is also a service, but an extremely selfish one, and therefore every more or less selfish service which people provide each other is more or less related to the service of hell, and can impossibly, as far as related to hell, have any value before God and all His heavens. Only a purely unselfish service is also a true and therefore purely heavenly service and has a true and perfect value before God and all His heavens.

If you serve each other, serve each other in love and true brotherliness, as it is the usual way in heaven! If someone requests a service from you, do it in all friendliness and love, and do not ask the service provider before delivering his service for the reward; since this is also done by the heathens, who do not know the true Father in heaven and have learned their customs more from animals than from God!

If somebody has provided you with a good service, you should not ask and say: "Friend, what do I owe you?", but you should reward your friend for the good delivered service in the best possible manner, according to your strength out of all love and joy of your heart! If he, who provided the good service to you, notices it, he will hug you and say: "Noble friend, I have only provided a very small service to you and you reward me too generously! See, a tenth of it is more than sufficient, and even this I accept only as proof of your brotherly heart which is so dear to me!"

If the service provider will talk to his service lord in such a manner with true and life-deep feelings, will not the servant and the employer become immediately true heavenly brothers?! Very much so, and thereby the true kingdom of God will come to you and heavenly rule over you with the scepter of light and all mercy.

7.5 About humility

Now comes another very important field of life, whereupon one only can reach truly the full rebirth of the spirit in his soul, which is life's truest triumph and highest end goal. This field is completely contrary to pride and arrogance and is called humility.

In each soul lays the same feeling of highness and ambition, which at the slightest opportunity and reason only too easily ignites into an all destructive raging passion and cannot be damped or rather completely extinguished, until it has consumed the offending victims. However, by this horrible passion, the soul becomes so damaged and material, that she becomes many times less suitable for an inner, spiritual perfection – than the glowing hot sand of the great desert of Africa to quench a thirst!

By the passion of the wretched arrogance the soul finally herself is transformed into a glowing desert sand, in which not one wretched little moss plant can grow, never mind any other more juicy and more blessed plant. This is the soul of a haughty person! Its wild fire singes and burns everything from the ground which is noble, good and true in life, and thousand times thousands of years will pass, until the sand desert of Africa will change in friendly and blissful fields. It will take for the whole sea many times to drive its floods over it!

Look at a proud king who was offended by his neighbor about any small matter! His soul is getting more and more into the wildest fire; from his eyes flames of rage are spraying, and the irrevocable resolution is: "The most dreadful revenge to the offender who forgot nobleness!" And a most disastrous war whereby hundreds of thousands must allow themselves to be killed in the most wretched manner for their proud and wanton king is the well-known and sad result of it. With great pleasure does the rage inflamed king overlooks from his tent the most insane battles and murders and rewards proudly each raging soldier with gold and gemstones, who was able to inflict the greatest and most sensitive damage to the opponent.

If such a king has robbed his insulter of nearly everything with his overwhelming power, it is by far not enough for him! He wants to see him tortured in front of him in the most gruesome manner! No imploring or begging is of any use. And even if the insulter has died in front of the king's proud eyes under the most painful tortures, on top of it his flesh will be cursed in the most horrible manner and scattered as food for the ravens, and never will any remorse enter the diamond heart of such a king, but the rage or the glowing desert of Africa remains, bringing continuously the most fearsome death to everyone who ever dares not to show the highest honor to the place where the proud king was standing.

Such a king has of course still a soul; but how does it look like? I say to you: worse than the most glowing spot of the great sand desert of Africa! Do you think that such a soul can be transformed into a fruit garden of the heavens of God? I say to you: A thousand times sooner will the desert of Africa produce the most marvelous dates, figs and grapes, than such a soul only the smallest drop of heavenly love!

Therefore, all of you beware above all about haughtiness; since nothing in the world destroys the soul more than the rage-snorting haughtiness and pride! An always present thirst for revenge is its companion, just like the everlasting and unquenchable thirst for rain is the continues companion of the great, glowing sand desert of Africa, and all animals putting their feet on its ground, will also soon be seized by the same plague, just as the servants of the proud king finally becomes also tremendously proud and revenge-thirsty. Who is a servant of pride, must in the end become proud himself. How could a servant of the proud be, then also very proud?!

Humility is primarily promoted by serving. Often, the more subordinated a service appears, the more suitable it is for the true development of life. Humility itself is nothing else than the increasingly and stronger condensation of life in itself, while haughtiness is a loose formation and a scattering into infinity and finally a complete loss of life, which we can call the second or the spiritual death.

In haughtiness all good serving has come to an end and therefore also all further development of life. If with the development of life a haughty ruling over others would be required, surely such a order would be created by God, that every person has an unlimited right to rule; but since this is against God eternal order, every person and angel must take up the apprenticeship of serving and finally find in the everlasting always increasing and expanding way of serving the highest joy and bliss.

Without serving there actually does not exist any life, no durable continuation of it, no happiness, no blessedness and no love, no wisdom and no joy of life, neither here nor in the beyond; and who thinks about heaven without any service, full of laziness and full of idle revelry, is grossly mistaken!

Actually, because of it, the most blest spirits of the highest heaven obtain a strength and power which resembles God, to provide Him and all people already here on this trial-world for life with a good-quality service. For what other purpose would be the possession of an even creative strength and power useful?! Does one then need strength and wisdom to do nothing?! If their work and usefulness is already of an indescribable importance for this world, how great must be their importance for the spiritual world and from it for the whole of infinity?

Christ surely has not come to us to make idlers from us, or to teach us to only carry out agriculture or cattle breeding or similar, but to make competent workers for the great vineyard of heaven form us. His teaching to us is aimed firstly to truly perfect us in the field of our inner life, and secondly, that we as self life-perfected beings can become, already here and especially one day in the beyond, in His Kingdom, the most competent and strongest workers for Him.

This is His final goal and he said to us: "Be active only here; one day in the beyond in My kingdom you will be able to revel with the best food and wine to eternity and rest and gawk at the marvels of God!"

Yes, you will have to marvel about the magnificence of God forever, but not without action; since it will actually depend on you, to increase the wonders of heaven and to make them continuously more marvelous and more divine!

He wants all His thoughts and ideas to become only through us a full reality, already here for soul, heart and spirit of our brothers and sisters, and in the beyond regarding all the great realities from their inner most spiritual sphere of origin up to their most outer material development, and from there to the repeated return to a increased, pure and independent spiritual, perfected life. And for that, friend, infinitively much time, patience and a great activity is required and an equally great and all-encompassing wisdom and strength!

How can a person protect himself against this most evil passion, since the seed for it is present in every soul and quite often has already reached a usury climax in children? Only through humility is this possible!

And therefore poverty is so predominantly large in comparison with richness of the people, to keep haughtiness always on a sharp rein. Just try to put a king's crown on the poorest beggar, and you will soon be convinced, how his earlier meekness and patience has evaporated with lightening speed. And therefore it is a very good thing, that there exists only a very few kings and a great number of modest beggars.

Every soul has, hereditary from God, whose idea and will she is, a feeling of highness, which presence one can already notice by the shyness of children. The feeling of shyness of children is a sensation of the soul, when she begins to feel herself, by the mute expression of discontent, since the soul as something spiritual sees herself trapped in a cumbersome and unmanageable flesh, which she cannot get rid of without pain. The more tender and sensitive the body of a soul, the stronger will be her feeling of shyness. If a right educator understands to lead this feeling, that cannot be eliminated, to the right modesty, he creates from this feeling a protective spirit and places it on the way, on which it easily can reach an early spiritual perfection; but only a little skew guidance of this hereditary feeling can immediately transfigure into haughtiness and pride.

To guide the feeling of shyness into the so called child-ambition is completely wrong; since then a child immediately begins to think he is better than others. It is easily offended and hurt and therefore cries bitterly; with this crying it expresses clearly that its feeling of highness is violated by someone.

If now weak and very shortsighted parents of the offended child try to calm it by, even if only apparently, call for accountability and punishment of the offender against their child, they have already placed the first seed in the child for quenching its thirst for revenge; and if the parents continue to calm the child in the same manner, they often create a devil for themselves and for many other people. But if the parents are clever and from early on show the child always the greater value in other people and children and in so doing guide the feeling of shyness into a right modesty, they will raise their children into angels, who will later serve as true examples of life for others, similar to the most beautiful stars shining in the night of the earthly life, and will revive them with their gentleness and patience.

Since children seldom receive such upbringing, by which their spirit will be awaken in their soul, the adult person reaching a purer recognition must above all attend to it, that he with all his strength makes the true and right humility his own. Before not eradicating the last drop of the feeling of highness, he cannot either here nor in the beyond pass over into a complete perfection of a purely spiritual heavenly life.

One should examine himself, if his meekness is completely perfected, should ask his heart if he still can be offended by anything, and if he can easily forgive his greatest offenders and pursuers from the bottom of his heart. One should do good to them who harmed him, and should not have any desire for any worldly magnificence. If one feels good about to be the smallest among the smallest, to serve everyone with everything, if one can do all this without sadness and grief, that one is already an inhabitant of the highest heaven of God and will remain as such forever, because through such just humility, a soul does not only becomes one with her spirit, but also to the greatest part of the material body.

Therefore, such a person will not feel nor taste the death of the body, since the entire ethereal part of the body – as the actual living natural body – has already become immortal with her soul and his spirit.

By the physical death only the lifeless shadow-part will be separated from the soul, which cannot cause the soul any fear and no further pain, because everything with an alive feeling of the body has become united with the soul, and therefore such a perfected person, after the separation of the anyway always insensible and therefore dead, outer shadow-body, will not feel anything, just as someone cannot feel anything when cutting his hair or fingernails of his body. What in the body never had a sense of feeling can also not have a feeling when the soul completely exits the body, because everything alive in the body and with a sense of feeling has already earlier become completely united with the soul and now forms one being with her, and will never be separated from her.

You have now seen what the right humility is, and what it is able to do, and therefore in future you will have to give a lot of attention to this virtue! Who, with great loyalty, follows what I have said to you, will convince himself that these easy understandable words, given without any oratorical, empty splendor, are not originating from man, but from God. And who lives and acts accordingly, walks on the right path to the true most inner, spiritual life's perfection.

7.6 About mercy

Always be merciful even towards the great sinners and criminals against your and against the divine laws! It is possible for an ill soul to commit a sin, but never for a healthy soul.

Who of you people can judge and punish a soul because she was violating one of God's commandments, since you are all standing under the same law?! One of the God's laws explicitly states, that you should not judge anyone! If you judge one of your neighbors who have sinned against divine laws, you also sin in the same measure against His law! But how can you as being a sinner yourself, judge and condemn another sinner?! Don't you know, that, when condemning your soul sick bother to hard atonement, you have served a double condemning judgment on yourself, which one day, if not under circumstances already here, will be fulfilled?!

When somebody is a sinner, he should resign as a judge; because if he judges someone, he judges himself into downfall twofold, from which he will recover more difficult than he who was judged and condemned by him. Can a blind man ever lead someone else and put him on the right path?! Or can one deaf person tell another deaf person something about the harmonic effects of music, as it was practiced in the purest form by David? Or can one disabled person say to another: "Come here, you poor man, I will take you to the inn!?" Will not soon both slip and fall into a ditch?!

Hence, remember this above all, not to judge anybody, and make sure that also those who one day will be under your watch take this to their hearts! Because by practicing this teaching you will make angels out of people, but through non-observance you will create devils and judges against yourselves.

It is true, nobody on this earth is perfect; however, the one who is more perfect in his mind and heart, should be the guide and doctor of his ill brothers and sisters, and the strong should carry the weak, otherwise the weak succumbs with the weak, and both will not make any progress!

Our way to judge will always remain the way of the world, and it will be difficult to ever completely crush the hard, diamond-like head of the dragon of tyranny, because for this very reason the earth is a test world for God's future children. But among us it should not continue, since among us the heavens are strewing fruits filled with plentiful seed kernels.

If you enjoy the fruits of His zeal now, do not forget to strew the leftover seed kernels copiously as possible into the hearts of your brothers and sisters, so that it can grow and carry plentiful and healthy new fruit! Act accordingly and you will as if out of yourself create life and receive the perfection of the everlasting life as shown to you right now! After this act of laying-on of hands it is given to you to follow and act accordingly in the most precise manner.

7.7 About repent and confession

Whoever recognizes his mistakes and repents is forgiven forever, and whoever then turns to God is doubly forgiven! But whoever recognizes his mistakes, but keeps them in his nature, he is not forgiven, even if he came to God a hundred times!

We should always be faithful to our position, act well and just – but never forget for an instant that those over whom we perform our duty are completely equal to us in birth and are thus our brothers. True love for your neighbor can be learnt through the true love that you have for God and His little children.

When it is necessary, make use of your reputation and the honor of your position, but you yourselves be full of humility and love, and your judgment over your brothers and sisters who have gone astray will always be just according to His order!

Whoever does not get rid of every smallest mote of arrogance will in the future not have God's kingdom revealed to him in the spirit, and he will not go there before he has removed the very last mote of arrogance from himself!

However, concerning the repent and confession before the priests, this works only if the priests are not wicked and thus completely objectionable, because they do not improve the people, but they only make the people to persist in their sins, until their end.

It is a good thing when a weak person, whose soul is sick, will voluntarily and honestly confess his weaknesses and faults to someone with a healthy soul, who is stronger than him, because the healthy person who is strong of light can then out of true neighborly love easily convey to him the real way by which the soul of the weak fellowman can become stronger and healthy. In this way, a person can be a real savior of souls.

The confession of sins alone will not purify a person from its sins, no more than a physically sick person, who will become healthy only by telling the doctor about his disease and how he has caught it, even if he does it in all sincerity. That one should listen to the advice of the doctor, who is wise and has much knowledge, and then one must follow the advice faithfully and avoid everything in the future that was the cause of his disease.

So it is also good when in a community every brother knows the other, his strong as well as his weak points, so that, concerning the soul, and also physically, one can and want to support the other according to the full truth. However, the one who does not want to tell anything because he thinks that with his confession he might offend anyone should not be provoked by anybody to confess his weaknesses.

But if anyone among you is wise, and his spirit reveals to him the weaknesses of the weak and fearful brother, then the wise one should give him privately a good advice and assist him by word and deed to help him out of his hidden need. Then his reward will not be kept away from him.

However, let everyone have his free will and force no one, for now you know that every moral compulsion is completely contrary to God's eternal order.

But you should not treat the weak brother who trustingly has been sincere to a stronger one among you, with a threatening face as from a judge, but always openly tell the truth to him with all love and friendliness, and also convey to him the means by which he easily and safely can be healed. Then he will not be discouraged and will be a grateful student of the free truth. But when you will approach him with all kinds of sermons of penance, you will not only accomplish little or nothing with him, but you will make him more miserable than he ever was before.

7.8   About real strength

Adam and his first descendents had neither tents nor huts nor comfortable houses. The ground of the Earth and a shady tree was their all, and they spent very many nights under the open sky and were healthy and strong. They did not have even a cover for their body; a wreath of fig leaves to cover their private parts was their entire clothing, and they all reached an age of several hundred years! But now people have discovered all sorts of comforts of life and have created many hundred thousands of paradises for a lost earthly one, and now reaching the age of a hundred has become a miracle!

Look, the effeminacy of man is to blame, who distance themselves from the nature of this world, which has the designation in all things to bear the people and to feed them and to keep them strong and healthy. Whoever is overcome by sleep can rest very well on a pillow of stone; if the stone beneath his head annoys him, then the person is no longer tired or in need of rest, and then he can stand up again and go to work!

Soft beds make people soft and take away the necessary strength of their limbs, and a too long sleep weakens the soul and the muscles of the body. The nature of a person is like an infant whom nothing feeds as well as the mother's breast; and those children who received food from the breast of the strong mother – assuming that she is as healthy and unspoiled as Eve – become as strong as giants and the battle with a lion will not tire them out.

To the same extent the nature of this Earth is a true mother's breast for man, if they do not distance themselves from it through all sorts of unnecessary softeners. But once the people have distanced themselves from this great mother's breast and isolated themselves from her strong influence, and then if they ever have to come to a breast that is rich in milk, they act in the same way as a grown man if he has to drink the milk from a mother. He is so disgusted he could throw up. What strengthened him as a child and fed him in the best way makes him sick and nauseous as an adult, who has long grown away from his mother's breast.

Now, man cannot always drink on his mother's breast to get strength and life for his muscles, but he should never distance himself too much from the breast of Mother Earth if he wants to become healthy, strong and old in the body.

Moses said: "Honor your father and mother, that your days may be long and healthy on the Earth!"

With this Moses not only described the biological father and mother, but just as well the Earth and its constant life-giving power. Man should not turn his back on this, but instead keep it in high respect, and he will receive every blessing for that which Moses physically prophesied. The respect for the physical father and mother is good and necessary when the circumstances are accordingly; but Moses prophesied the word of God, then it must also have a general and uninterrupted effect like the sunlight!

If Moses" prophecy is only limited to the fact that only those who respect their parents have to maintain a long life and health on the Earth, then things obviously look very bad for those who have often lost this in the cradle and were then brought up by strangers! How should they respect their true parents whom they have never known?!

Many children are often found on paths and streets; cruel mothers have conceived them in their lust and thrown them out somewhere soon after their birth. Such foundlings are often taken in by some warm-hearted and compassionate person and looked after; they then owe all their love and respect to these people. Moses says nothing about such adoptive parents, only about really true parents!

But now the well-brought up foundling cannot possibly honor his true parents, because he firstly does not know them at all, and even if he did, he would secondly truly have no obligation before God or before all people to respect them, who conceived him through sinful lust and who, when he was born, immediately gave him over to death. But because such a person then according to Moses cannot possibly love and respect his true parents, would he then have no claim on Moses" prophecy? Oh, would this then be very pretty indeed and would it be terrible as the word of God!

And then there are parents who bring their children up in all things that can only be called bad. Already in the cradle they plant a genuine satanic arrogance in them and teach them to be hard and insensitive to everyone; such tiger parents teach their children at an early age to be cheeky, liars and deceivers! Should Moses really have meant his commandment for such children who respect their vicious parents with all badness and evil because the parents want this from their children?

What do the children of thieves, robbers and murderers really owe their parents? They can only naturally honor their parents if they are the same as their parents to a very great degree and do what their parents always do, like: through theft, robbery and murder of foreign travelers! Can Moses" prophecy really apply effectively to such children as well?

The only somewhat clear world reason must tell you that such a prophecy along with the Law of Moses would be a scandal of the first category for all divine wisdom! How can God, the highly wise, give a law as a consequence of which even an angel in a fleshly body would have to owe love and all honor to parents who incarnated from the lowest hell?!

So on the one hand it is clear and proven that everything that Moses said and decided is the pure word of God and therefore can eternally hide no nonsense in itself; but on the other hand, if one examines and observes Moses" Law in the old familiar and foolish way, as it has been examined and observed so far, it must be the most obvious nonsense before the judge's seat of all better human reason!

Wherein lays the reason then that the Law of Moses, as it has been observed so far, must be nonsense despite the purely divine origin? It lays in the powerful misunderstanding of what Moses showed mainly with this Law, the general parents of the great nature, namely the Earth, as the created world for the human race as father, and its Nature, from which countless children of all types and sort are born, as the true mother! These original parents should constantly be honored and obeyed by man, and his back should never be turned to them in an effeminate way. Only then he will receive a long life in a healthy body and also a true well-being.

A diligent person can also learn from these old parents the most goodness, greatness and truth, and build a great ladder on which the original father Jacob saw the angels of heaven climbing up and down. Whoever seriously researches Nature will force many blessings to come into the light for himself and for his brothers for their well-being.

7.9 *About faith*

All the people are the same. They want to see signs, to believe. One is blessed if believes, although on account of the signs. He, who nevertheless does not believe in spite of the signs, has sunk into death. But in future only those people shall attain bliss who believes just on account of the truth of His Word, without signs, living in accordance with it. These shall then discover the only living sign within themselves, called eternal life, and this no one shall be able to take from them.

If a man were to live in accordance with inner pure love and then came upon such truth, having no more doubt in his truth, he then could say unto one of those surrounding mountains: arise and cast thyself into the sea. And the mountain would rise and cast itself into the sea.

But since no such truth resides in your heart, you cannot work such deeds and on top of that you wonder many times head over heels that Jesus Christ, who is imbued with such truth in all fullness, performed deeds before his followers, which can be accomplished only through the might of the innermost living truth.

Only within such truth does faith, which in man is the right hand of the spirit, become living in power-action, and the arm of the spirit reaches far and performs great things.

If through such truth you shall have sufficiently strengthened your spiritual arms, then you shall be doing what Christ have done before us, and besides that you shall see that this is much easier than to lift a stone off the ground with the hand of your body, and cast it several paces before you.

Therefore, we should live in accordance with His teaching. Be doers and not just idle hearers and admirers of His Words, teachings and deeds, and you shall receive within yourselves that which now you so highly admire in him.

7.10 *About revelation and the true prophet*

Goodness and truth are the same, whether a man discovers it by active searching or whether it is revealed to him directly by God; for finding the truth oneself is also a revelation from above, but an indirect one and the means for it is active searching.

Through such research the soul frees itself from the rough bond of matter and awakens thereby for moments the divine Spirit in itself, or it comes more into the living centre of its heart. There flows God's light and compassion constantly and ceaselessly and likewise creates for the soul life and spiritual growth, as the sun fills the furrows of the earth with light and warmth and thereby awakes, maintains and encourages the life and flourishing of the plants until a free, independent and fully ripe fruit is created from the plant, whose own life is no longer dependent on the plant, but persists on itself.

When the soul comes into the mentioned living centre of the heart in true, lively moments, it has also reached the revelation of the Spirit out of God in every human heart and can do nothing else but find the eternally unchanged truth from God in itself. And that is an indirect revelation and differs from the direct revelation only in that God, at the occasion of great darkness of nations, awakens suitable people unaware about their prophetic role and leads their soul into the centre of life in order to create again an eye-opening light for other blind people.

And there is another difference between the indirect and direct revelation, and this consists of this: The indirect revelation gives the seeker only a correct light on a matter which he particularly wants to understand. It is like a lamp with which one can illuminate dark room quite brightly. The direct revelation is like the sun on the brightest midday, whose powerful light illuminates the whole world in all its great and little trenches.

The direct revelation is not only valid only for the people to whom it is given, but for all people, and immediately for the nation to which the prophet belongs; but because there are genuine and true prophets called by God, we can also easily imagine that there will also be false ones, and for the following reasons which are easy to understand:

A true prophet must come to a sort of esteem among his fellow people; for his prophecies and also his deeds as proof of the divinity of his awakening, He must create a certain respect among the ordinary everyday person – whether they like the prophecies, or not, and whether they correspond with his earthly interests, or not. A prophet grows among people of better sense without his will into an unreachable giant and can never escape the certain pious respect and reverence, no matter how humble he is and must be otherwise.

Now, other worldly people see that, whose reason is often very inventive; for there has never been a lack of snake like cleverness among the children of the world. These worldly people also want a reputation and an easily visible earthly gain. They begin to study and often invent things with the help of Satan and make seemingly wise statements so that the lay people do not know how to distinguish in the end between what is true and genuine and what is false and evil.

But how can one nevertheless tell a false prophet from a genuine one? Quite easily: in their fruit! For one cannot gather grapes and figs from thorns and thistles!

The genuine prophet will never and impossibly be selfish, and any arrogance will be foreign to him. He will probably gratefully accept whatever good and noble hearts give him; but he will never demand fees of anyone because he knows that this is an abomination to God, and because God can keep His servants very well!

But the false prophet will allow himself to be paid for every step and deed and for every so-called divine act for the simulated and lied good of humanity. The false prophet will thunder on about the judgment of God and even judge in the name of God with fire and sword; but the genuine prophet will judge no-one, but only advise the sinner to repent and will make no difference between large and small and between respected and non-respected people. For only God means anything to him and God's word – everything else is a vain madness for him.

There will never be a contradiction between the true prophet's speech and its actions; but bring speech of the false prophet into the light and his actions will be crawling with contradictions. No-one can ever offend the true prophet, he will bear everything like a lamb, whatever the world may do to him; he will only rise up in fiery power against lies and arrogance and beat them down.

The false prophet is constantly a deadly enemy of every truth and every better progress in thoughts and in deeds. No-one but he should know the ultimate truth or have any high spiritual experience so that everyone is always and in all things forced to seek advice from him (most of the time in exchange for money).

The false prophet thinks only about himself; God and His order are annoying and laughable things in which he has not even the smallest spark of faith, therefore he can make a god out of wood and stone with the lightest conscience in the world, however he likes. Then such a god can easily work wonders for the thoroughly blind people through the hands of the false prophet!

7.11 Why to return good for evil?

What good can you achieve by returning evil for evil? If you were to cook a meal which in itself is tasteless, will you gain anything by adding gall and aloe, instead of seasoning it with salt, milk and honey? If you add something still better to an already good meal, then certainly no one will call you stupid, but if you make an already bad meal worse with still more inferior ingredients, where is the man who will not say to you: "Look at what the fool is doing!"

Much more is it with men! If you return them evil for evil, then ask yourself whether their wickedness is improved. If you return good for evil, then you shall soften the evil in your brother heart and perhaps in the end make a good brother of him.

If a master has a servant to whom he entrusts much, while the latter, knowing the master's goodness, commits a sin against him and therefore merits punishment, and being called to account for his faithlessness, meets his master with rage and vituperates against him, will this soften the master towards his servant? I tell you it will not! The master shall only get angry over the faithless servant, have him bound and thrown in jail.

If however the servant sees that the master is about to treat him harshly, and he falls down before him to confess his transgression remorsefully and gently, and lovingly asks his forgiveness, will the master treat him as formerly? Through the servant's gentle contrition the master shall not only become gentle and pliable but shall do good to his servant besides.

Therefore, do not repay evil for evil, if you want all to become good. If however you are going to judge and punish those who have sinned against you, then you shall in the end all turn evil and there shall be no more proper love and goodness in any of you.

It is in itself very clear that one should not behave too friendly in front of an arch-devil person, in order not to give him more opportunity to let his evilness grow and become always more evil than he was before. In this case, a continuous indulgence would mean nothing else than a true support for the too strongly growing evilness of the enemy. That is why God gave us the commandment that we should be submitted to the worldly authority, whether it is mild or severe.

So if someone has such terrible enemy, he should go to a worldly judge and report it to him. Then the judge will drive out the evilness of the person who became arch-devil.

If only physical chastisement will not help, it will finally help with the sword. And so it is the same with the slap. If you receive it from a less evil person who was tempted to it by a sudden impulse of his temper, do not resist, so that he will become milder by the fact that you did not slap him in return and you will then again easily become good friends without worldly judge.

If someone comes to you in full anger with a murderous slap, then you also have the fullest right to resist. Look, if it were not so, the Lord would not have told us to shake off the dust from our feet in a place with people who not only do not want to accept us, but moreover mock us and threaten us with all kinds of persecution.

With the preaching about neighborly love, God did not abolish the might and the authority of the sword in the least, but He made it milder as long as the enmity among people does not reach the degree which one could very rightfully call "hellish".

7.12 *About clairvoyance through introspection*

This practice is not about how one can acquire special, miraculous or magic qualities, nor will the recipe be given to only strife for these, but the way will be shown here how to overcome the multiple doubts of the heart which the soul feels as long as he has not loosened the bands of his flesh. This is the true goal: to be independent from the flesh with all its lusts, doubts and errors in order to feel good in the actual, real and true world, and to be completely free.

It is obvious that when the constricting shackles of the flesh become looser, the life of the soul must of itself completely become noticeable. And all those who hear His Word, but who further on do not perceive anything of that inner life of the soul, are still completely stuck in their fleshly bonds. They are hearers but not doers of the Word.

Everyone who will cast off his shackles of the flesh receives a clearer view on people and nature. At the beginning in such a way, that he only thinks that his ability of perception is becoming much sharper. But it actually means that the spirit is stirred, receiving more freedom of movement. Then man should take the habit to look into himself, this means to recognize the images that his spiritual eye can see, independently from his physical eyes and can observe. Then, when he stands in the love for God and continues to build on that basis, he will quickly acquire the quality of the Spirit which you call "clairvoyance". But this is not a magic quality, but a very natural one of the soul, against which he can of course close off himself just like you can close off yourself in the body against the development of various qualities.

During sickness the connection between soul and body becomes often looser. The clairvoyance which then exists by the weakness of the body is a kind of unhealthy clairvoyance by which many things appear that are not correct. The life of the soul in a world that is completely strange to him is nothing unusual with sick people, and the many imaginations that appear by that are nothing else but corresponding images of the world of the soul. Corresponding images because the language in which the Spirit speaks to the soul are not words but only complete ideas while words can only communicate those ideas with difficulty.

The development of the ability to understand the language of the Spirit – at least according to the Word – as the language of correspondences, is not only useful during lifetime, but even necessary because otherwise the soul will, after the death of his body, feel like a stranger in the spiritual kingdom, coming into a completely strange country in which he cannot understand the language and where he can only make himself understandable with great difficulty. Only with this difference: that the inhabitants of that country understand the stranger but he does not understand the inhabitants who first have to adopt again to the laborious shackles of the souls" life to be familiar again with the laborious physical language which became unusual and by which one can only make contact by means of words but not by a series of thoughts.

This is why spiritually advanced people often regret the impossibility to express their feelings in sufficiently clear words, or the impossibility to set out, through writing or speaking, the flow of their thoughts as quickly as the spirit shows them to the soul. All this would not be possible if that language of the spirit in quick images and series of ideas would not exist.

So, there is more than being able to communicate in word and writing, and let thus no one believe that a very highly developed language or a highly developed orators talent is the most brilliant gift through which the soul of man can communicate, for these are only very weak outflows of the inner striving of the Spirit to share with the soul of what lays most perfectly hidden in the Spirit. So let no one believe that he has achieved something special when he is considered a master in this outer communication. He is only a poor bungler compared to the richness of the inner master that does not display its talents to the outer.

Coming back to the habit to look into himself, first of all one have to let nothing troubling him. Whatever time shall present, that shall be seized upon. But today's and tomorrow's time shall deliver nothing or little other than ourselves, and therefore we shall have no need for special preparations.

For truly I tell you: nothing is of greater benefit for the whole man than introspection at a precise time. Whoever wishes to become acquainted with himself and his powers must sometimes search and contemplate his within.

Some do not know how to go about this introspection. Just relax and think quietly and exclusively attentive at your actions and the well-known will of God and whether you have complied with it at different times of your life, then you have contemplated within yourself and have made it increasingly difficult for Satan to enter your heart. For Satan seeks eagerly through all kinds of external meaningless trickery to prevent a person from such introspection.

Once a man has acquired through practice a certain accomplishment in introspection, he easily discovers within himself the traps Satan has set him and is then able to properly destroy and eliminate them and energetically take precautions against all further deceitfulness of this enemy. Satan is quite aware and is, therefore, busily occupied with engaging the soul in all kinds of diverting trickery and then finds it quite easy, unnoticed behind the scene, to lay a snare for the soul in which it gets so entangled that it can no longer manage introspection, and this is very bad. Thereby the soul is more and more separated from its Spirit, which it can no longer awaken, and that is already the beginning of the second death within man.

Now, you know wherein introspection consists. Practice this quietly from now on and do not let any external thing disturb you. For Satan will certainly not refrain from diverting you through one or the other external spectacle. Remember that I have foretold you this and return again quickly to your within!

7.13 *About praying*

Pray in every need and adversity, with natural words in your heart, to God, and you will not pray in vain. When you ask Him something do not use many words, and absolutely no ceremonies, but pray very quietly, in the secret love chamber of your heart: "Our loving Father, who lives in Heaven, Your name be sanctified always and forever. May your Kingdom of Life, Light and Truth come to us and stay with us. May your only holy and righteous Will be done on this Earth among us people, in the same manner as in Your Heavens among Your perfected angels. But on this Earth, give us our daily bread. Forgive us our sins and weaknesses, as we will always forgive those who sinned against us. Let no temptations come over us that we cannot resist, and free us in this way from all evil in which man can fall as a result of too strong enticements of this world and its evil spirit. For to You, o Father in Heaven, belongs all might, all power, all strength and all glory which fills all Heavens from eternity to eternity."

In this way, everyone should pray in his heart, and then his prayer will be heard if it was meant in all seriousness. But not only with the mouth, but truthfully and lively in his heart, for God is in Himself a purest Spirit, and so He should be worshipped in the spirit and in the full earnest truth.

When you are praying, you should not think that you can stir God to greater mercy towards a person, since He truly is endless more merciful than all the best and most loving people of the whole world together. It is better to submit faithfully this gospel to that person, out of the true foundation of love of your heart. Then they will hear it and will also conform themselves to its spirituality. And in this way you will also announce the gospel to those who are truly poor of spirit, which will be a great benefit for them.

All the other kind of prayer and rattling off of prayers does not help a person in the least, since usually such prayers have to be paid.

Praying for the deceased and the caring for their spiritual poverty is certainly a fruitful blessing for them. On the other hand, a costly paid-for prayer is for them a curse, from which they quickly are fleeing away and which they deeply despise.

Observe this well, for by that you will acquire true, great, mighty and grateful friends in the great world on the other side, who will not ever leave you, neither on this nor on the other side if ever you would be in need. Such friends will then be your true protective spirits and will always be concerned for the well being of their benefactors.

Do not look for any reward in this world for the little sacrifices that you made, perform all the things that you do out of true, inner love for God, your Father, then he will surely know and will prepare a true joyful return for His beloved children.

What use will it be to a person if he would possess all the treasures of the world, but thereby would suffer great harm to his soul? Therefore, always be concerned about treasures that cannot be eaten up by moths and cannot be corroded by rust, then that will always be the best for you.

Remember also this advice very well and observe it, then already on this Earth you will have a good existence, as well as the other people who will believe your words.

Long prayers has not only no value for God, but is an abomination to Him. To what purpose are those long prayers for God, the all wise One? If 1,000 of such praying men would pray during a 1,000 years, rattling off their long prayers to God, then God would listen those even less than to the braying of a hungry donkey, because such a prayer is no prayer but only the quacking of frogs in a swamp, for it has no purpose and no meaning, and will also never have one.

God in Himself is a Spirit of the highest wisdom and He has the very deepest and clearest mind, and is the eternal Truth Himself. So he, who wishes to pray to God effectively, must pray in spirit and truth. However, only the one, who is going into the quiet love chamber of his heart, and in it, will be worshipping and invoking God, will be praying in spirit and truth. And God, who perceives all hearts, will surely also see into your heart and recognize for sure how and for what you are praying and asking, and He will give you what you have so truly prayed for in spirit and in truth.

However, the complete true prayer consists in keeping God's commandments and, out of love for Him, acting according to His will. Whoever will pray like this prays truly and prays without ceasing. All the heavenly angels are praying to God without ceasing, because they always are doing the will of God. God does not want to be worshipped, honored and praised with psalms and psaltery, with harps, cymbals and trumpets, but only by your dynamic, fully zealous activity according to His word and His will.

If you look at God's works and you will continuously discover and recognize His love and wisdom in it, you will grow in love for Him by that, and you will become continuously wiser within yourself, then you also are truly praying, and you are giving true glory to God. All the other things, what you have understood until now by praying, are totally empty, void and without value for God.

As it is said before, the only true prayer consists of the sincerest love for God, the Father in heaven and equally for your fellowmen, who are your neighbors. Without this, all other prayers have no value before God. Jesus Christ never taught people to honor God with lips and keep their hearts cold. But since Samuel prayed audibly in front of the people, equally so several of the prophets, and because David sang to God the Lord his psalms and Salomon his High Song, the people came to empty lip prayer and to cold sacrifices.

However, before God such prayers and sacrifices are repulsive! Who cannot pray in the heart should rather not pray at all, so as to not behave improper before God. God did not give feet, hands, eyes, ears and lips to man to pray vainly and vacuously, but only the heart!

But, man still can pray with feet, hands, eyes, ears and lips; namely with feet if he goes to the poor and brings them assistance and consolation; with the hands if he grabs the needy under the arms; with the eyes if he loves looking at the poor; with the ears if it pleases him to listen to God's word actively and does not close them in front of the poor; and finally with the lips if it pleases him to talk to the poor, desolate widows and orphans in a comforting manner and according to his power and strength speaks a mitigating word on behalf of prisoners to those who often imprison innocent people, so that they can be released.

Thus man also prays with lips if he teaches the uneducated the true faith, the right recognition of God and all kinds of useful virtues. All this is then also a God pleasing prayer.

It is written that man should pray uninterruptedly, if he does not want to fall into temptation; but how foolish and completely clownish would it be, if God would insist on an incessant outer prayer from man! When would they perform a necessary work? But if you with hands, feet, eyes, ears and lips are constantly active and in your hearts always love God and your poor fellowmen, you pray truthfully and by action incessantly to God, Who therefore always will bless you and one day in the beyond will give you the most blissful, everlasting life!

Be truly reasonable and have a decent heart, do good deeds to everyone who needs your help! Yes, even do good to your enemies, and bless those who curse you! In this way, you will resemble God, for God let the sun to shine on the good and the bad, and His worst enemies are daily covered with good deeds from His all-powerful hand;

Therefore, if you pray, do not pray like the heathens and the Pharisees with their lips, using words formed by the fleshly tongue, but instead pray in the spirit and in truth, through living works and deeds of love towards your neighbor, then every word in God's name will be a true prayer, and God will always and without a doubt hear and respond to your pray!

7.14 About fasting

Christ did not abolish the old commandment of fasting. The one who fasts with the right attitude is indeed doing a good work in itself, for by sincerely fasting and praying to God, the soul becomes more free and spiritual. But only fasting and praying will save nobody, but only by doing the Will of the Father. But this Will can be done without the mentioned fasting and without the abstinence of certain foods and drinks.

The one who love God and practices true neighborly love is truly fasting, and that fasting is pleasing to God and is useful for the eternal life of man. He, who has much, let him also give much, and he, who has little, let also him share the little he has with his fellowman, who is still poorer than he is. Then he will gather treasures in Heaven. Giving in itself is already better than taking.

However, the one who truly wants to fast for God, so that it is useful for the eternal life of his soul, should, out of love for God and his fellowman, refrain from sinning, for sins are burdening the soul, so that it can only raise itself to God with difficulty.

The one who celebrates comfort and revelries, and who is deaf for the voice of the poor, is sinning against the commandment of fasting, and so also does every fornicator and adulterer.

If the sensuous forms of a young girl, or even of the woman which is married with another person, is attracting you and brings you into temptation, then turn away your eyes and restrain from the lusts of the body, then by this, you have truly fasted!

If someone has offended you and made you angry, then forgive him. Go to him and agree with one another, then you have validly fasted!

If you do good to the one who has done wrong to you, and bless the one who curses you, then you have truly fasted!

What goes into the mouth to feed and to strengthen the body does not defile man, but that what often comes out of the mouth, like calumny, slander, dirty talks, backbiting, cursing, false witnesses and all kinds of lies and blasphemy, are defiling man. And whoever does that is actually breaking the true fasting!

For truly, fasting means to deny oneself in everything, to take the appointed load on your shoulders, with patience and to follow Christ, for Christ is humble and patient with all his heart.

When you go out into the world in Christ's name and live among all kinds of foreign nations, then eat whatever will be set before you. But never eat and drink immoderately. Then you will fast the right way. All the other things are only superstition and a great foolishness of the people from which they have to be liberated.

7.15 *The hearers and the doers*

The spiritual Kingdom of Heaven is everywhere as endlessly extended as this endless physical universe of which you can see with your eyes. This Earth, the great sun, the moon and the stars you can see with your eyes (all of which are immense worlds, some of them thousands upon thousands million times larger than this Earth) all that taken together is, compared to the endlessly vast creation of the material world, in magnitude and vastness, not even as much as the smallest dewdrop compared to the immense ocean, which is so vast that a good sailor would need more than twice the age of Methuselah to sail over all of its area. However, the material world up to now, as much as has already been created, still has a limit, beyond which there exists an infinite, eternal space. Compared to the absolutely endless expansion, in all directions, the entire aforesaid creation of the whole material world is like a moment compared to eternity.

Thus, the spirit world is quite as endless as infinite space that does not end anywhere. Although space has nowhere an end in eternity and is thus truly endless in all directions, there is in its most endless depths and distances not a single spot where the spirit of God's wisdom and might is not as much present as now here, with you. The true children of God, who will excel in proper love for God, the holy Father from eternity, and also in pure love for their neighbors, in the great house of the Father, shall obtain the might and the power to forever fill the infinite space with more and more new creations.

However, you are still too ignorant and cannot grasp what I have now told you. But this I nevertheless tell you: No mortal eye can see nor ear hear and no earthly sense can ever grasp what beyond, in the Kingdom of Heaven, awaits those who become worthy of being called children of God.

For, before the eyes of true children of God, the globes, suns and moons shall be floating like glimmering dust. Therefore, do not be only hearers, but be doers of God's Word.

Only the deed will let you recognize whether the words I have spoken to you, and I am still speaking, are coming to you as an eternal truth.

But just as you let yourselves to be complete doers of God's Word – if you have an enlivening conviction as to who is He that has given you this teaching and commandment of love – you are also spurn on the deed of all those to whom you proclaim His Word, and the Word merely adheres to their brain, because this has no higher worth than the braying of a donkey.

Only when the Word penetrates the heart does it become live, taking hold of the will, which is the focus of love, driving the whole man unto action. Through such action a new man arises within the old and the Word actually becomes new flesh and blood.

Only this new man shall show you that these Words truly are of God, having today the same authority, power and effect as eternities of eternities ago, because everything you see, feel, smell, taste and hear is basically nothing other than God's Word.

He, who eternities ago, out of Himself, commanded the worlds, suns and moons to be, placing them in their extensive tracks, the Same is now placing you into new tracks of the eternal life.

* * *